THE CHURCH OF GOD IN CHRIST
PRESIDING BISHOP

Bishop J. Drew Sheard

"UNFINISHED BUSINESS"

"Jesus saith unto them, My meat is to do the will of him that sent me, and to finish his work." John 4:34, KJV

Evangelist Terri Hannett • Executive Director
Supervisor Barachias Irons • Chief Editor

Church Of God In Christ
PUBLISHING HOUSE

806 East Brooks Road, Memphis, Tennessee 38116
P. O. Box 161330, Memphis, Tennessee 38186
• **Toll Free:** 1-877-746-8578 | Fax: 901-743-1555
• **Website:** www.cogicpublishinghouse.net
• **Email:** sales@cogicpublishinghouse.net

FROM THE OFFICE OF THE PRESIDING BISHOP

Greetings in the name of our Lord and Savior, Jesus Christ.

In this time of rapid change, it is vitally important for blood washed individuals to actively participate in our churches and communities to assure our voices are heard and God is glorified.

We must remain "steadfast, unmovable, always abounding in the work of the Lord, forasmuch as ye know that your labor is not in vain in the Lord".

With that being said, I want you to know, we have "Unfinished Business" in upholding our Christian duties and engaging in constructive dialogue to address societal challenges and the continued advancement of the Kingdom of God.

The Power for Living curriculum is filled with scriptures that will encourage and motivate you to keep pressing your way in the things of the Lord.

I encourage you to share the Word of God on every occasion and live so God can use you, anywhere and anytime.

Sincerely,

J. Drew Sheard,

Presiding Bishop and Chief Apostle

Church Of God In Christ, Inc.

CHURCH OF GOD IN CHRIST, INC.
930 Mason St. | Memphis, TN 98126
Office: 901.947.9300 | Fax: 901.947.9327
www.COGIC.org

THE VOICE OF THE CHAIRMAN OF THE PUBLISHING BOARD

Blessings in the name of the Lord Jesus Christ,

The fact that you are reading this letter indicates that God has blessed you to experience another year of His grace and mercy. We often transition from one season to the next and sometimes take for granted the privilege God affords us to see a new year, a new season, and a new day. Thank God for our now and our next!

Our Presiding Bishop has ushered us into a new season this year, realizing that our church has "Unfinished Business." In John 4:34, Jesus, speaking to disciples, said, "My meat is to do the will of him that sent me, and to finish his work." Here, Jesus reminds his disciples of the purpose of their mission and that both planting spiritual seeds and collecting the harvest are valuable. And God wants us to know that if we expect to reap a harvest, we must first scatter the seed of the Good News of Christ to a dying and depleted world.

Understand that the seed has no flaws because it is God's Word. It holds much potential, but it can only be activated if it takes root in fertile soil. Our job as the church is to plant the seed of life into the heart of every person: "Go ye into all the world and preach the gospel to every creature" (Mark 16:15). Once these seeds are planted, our churches will grow: "The harvest truly is plenteous, but the labourers are few" (Matthew 9:37).

Sunday School is the foundational building block of our church. God's seed is cultivated during school on Sunday so we can face the world on Monday. We have an obligation to spread God's word so that His business may be accomplished here on earth.

I thank the thousands of loyal supporters of our literature who partner in God's mission of sharing the Good News to the world. We have work to do! I want to personally thank you for answering the call so that lives may be changed and transformed.

We are also in a time of political change. So, I ask that you continue to pray for the unity of our country and pray for God to manifest Himself in our lives and our churches in a new way. I ask that the Lord shift the winds of grace and favor in our direction so that we can experience Him as we have never experienced Him before. Church, let's do the work. We have unfinished business!

In His Service,
Bishop Uleses C. Henderson, Jr.
Chairman of the Publishing Board
Church Of God In Christ Inc.

THE VOICE OF MARKETING

Dear Saints,

Greetings in the matchless name of our Lord and Savior, Jesus Christ! I pray this letter finds you in good health and strengthened by God's unchanging grace. As we approach another season of celebration and reflection, I am reminded of God's faithfulness and His call to us to remain steadfast in the work of the Kingdom.

The theme for this year, **"Unfinished Business,"** compels us to look inward and upward as we commit ourselves to fulfilling the divine mandate given to each of us. Jesus reminds us in John 4:34, *"My food is to do the will of Him who sent Me, and to finish His work."* Just as our Savior found sustenance in obedience to God's purpose, so too must we press forward to complete the assignments He entrusted us.

In these challenging times, it is easy to grow weary or become distracted by the cares of life. Yet, the work of the Kingdom cannot wait. There are souls to save, broken hearts to mend, and communities to uplift. The business of love, justice, mercy, and evangelism remains unfinished, and God has chosen us—His Church—as vessels to carry out His will.

This is a clarion call to all of us:
- **To stay mission-minded** in advancing the Gospel.
- **To serve tirelessly** in our communities and congregations.
- **To build bridges of hope** where there is despair.
- **To finish the race** with the confidence that we have done the work He sent us to do.

Let us approach this season with renewed passion and unwavering faith. As we labor together, may we keep our eyes on the One who is the Author and Finisher of our faith.

I encourage you, beloved saints, to recommit yourselves to the work God has placed in your hands. Whether in your local church, family, or community, know your labor is not in vain. The harvest is plentiful, and the time to finish the work is now.

May the Holy Spirit empower us to persevere and complete the mission with joy and diligence. Thank you for your faithful service, your prayers, and your love for the body of Christ. Together, let us press forward, confident in the promise that He who began a good work in us will bring it to completion.

With great expectation for what God will do in and through us,

Yours in Christ,

Sandra S. Jones, B.S., MTh., PhD (c)
Chairman of Marketing (Board)
Senior Marketing/Sales Consultant
Church Of God In Christ Publishing House

QUARTERLY QUIZ

The questions on this page may be used in several ways: as a pretest at the beginning of the quarter; as a review at the end of the quarter; or as a review after each lesson. The questions are based on the Scripture text of each lesson (King James Version).

LESSON 1

1. What spiritual event was celebrated during this time (Acts 2:1)?

2. The people were so "_____ _____, they asked: 'Aren't all these who are speaking Galileans?'" (Acts 2:7).

LESSON 2

1. What type of punishment will God send to Judah and the palaces of Jerusalem (**Amos 2:5**)?

2. The people would ____ the ____ of the condemned in the house of their god (**Amos 2:8**).

LESSON 3

1. How did God respond to the people celebrating their feast days (**Amos 5:21**)?

2. Write the famous words of justice declared by the prophet Amos (**Amos 5:24**).

LESSON 4

1. What type of houses will be destroyed in **Amos 6:11?**

2. Amos declares that the people have changed righteousness into _____ (**Amos 6:12**).

LESSON 5

1. In **Amos 8:5**, the merchants would be glad when the new moon would be gone. Why?

_____

_____

2. The merchants cheated the poor by creating new "money" by making the _____ _____ and the _____ _____ (**Amos 8:5**).

LESSON 6

1. The rich were not open to hearing Micah's judgment from God against them. What was their response to Micah (**Micah 2:6**)?

_____

_____

2. The rich were about to evicted from their land—true or false (**Micah 2:10**)?

_____

_____

LESSON 7

1. In **Micah 3:7**, what will happen to the lips of the various "speakers of truth"?

_____

_____

2. Micah prophesied that Zion and Jerusalem will experience _____ (**Micah 3:12**).

_____

_____

LESSON 8

1. Why do you think the Lord asked the people to testify against Him in **Micah 6:3**?

_____

_____

2. What does the Lord require of His people (**Micah 6:8**)?

_____

_____

LESSON 9

1. The _____ will be _____ by what God will do (**Micah 7:16**).

_____

_____

2. What image is used in **Micah 3:17** to describe how the nations will respond to God's movement?

_____

_____

LESSON 10

1. Why was God displeased (**Isaiah 59:15b**)?

_____

_____

2. God saw no ____ and no _____ to intervene for the people (**Isaiah 59:16**).

_____

_____

LESSON 11

1. The Lord instruct Jeremiah to stand at the _____ of the Lord's house, the temple (**Jeremiah 7:2**).

_____

_____

2. Name the city that God challenged the people to visit and see where He allowed the temple to be destroyed (**Jeremiah 7:12**).

_____

_____

LESSON 12

1. Write one of the just actions of the righteous father in **Ezekiel 18:7**.

_____

_____

2. Complete the following Scripture: "For I have no pleasure_____

_____" (**Ezekiel 18:32**).

LESSON 13

1. Name the prophet that God speaks to in **Zechariah 7:8**.

_____

_____

2. The prophet proclaims in **Zechariah 7:9** that the Lord expects the people to do what?

_____

_____

LESSON 14

1. What type of messenger will be sent to the temple (**Malachi 3:1**)?

_____

_____

2. State the characteristic God shares about Himself in **Malachi 3:6**.

_____

_____

ADULT QUARTERLY

SUMMER QUARTER 2025

JUNE • JULY • AUGUST

Unit 1 • Amos Rails Against Injustice
JUNE

1	Gifts of Languages	9
8	Judgment on Israel and Judah	16
15	God is Not Fooled	22
22	Rebuked for Selfishness	29
29	God Will Never Forget	35

Unit 2 • Micah Calls for Justice Among Unjust People
JULY

6	No Rest for the Wicked	41
13	No Tolerance for Corrupt Leaders and Prophets	48
20	Justice, Love and Humility	54
27	God Shows Clemency	60

Unit 3 • Advocates of Justice for All
AUGUST

3	Our Redeemer Comes	66
10	A Chance to Be Just	72
17	A Call for Repentance	79
24	God Demands Justice	85
31	Return to A Just God	91

LESSON 1 • JUNE 1, 2025

GIFT OF LANGUAGES

BIBLE BASIS: ACTS 2:1–7, 12; 1 CORINTHIANS 14:13–19

BIBLE TRUTH: The need for finding a common understanding is necessary whether people are speaking in different native languages as in Acts 2 or unknown spiritual languages as in 1 Corinthians 14.

MEMORY VERSE: "What is it then? I will pray with the spirit, and I will pray with the understanding also: I will sing with the spirit, and I will sing with the understanding also" (1 Corinthians 14:15).

LESSON AIM: By the end of the lesson, your students will: DISCOVER how the Holy Spirit helped people communicate in both different native and spiritual languages; EMPATHIZE with people in situations in which language inhibits communication; and FIND ways to communicate with diverse people to foster common understanding.

BACKGROUND SCRIPTURE: Amos 2:4–8; Psalm 75—Read and incorporate the insights gained from the Background Scriptures into your study of the lesson.

LESSON SCRIPTURE

ACTS 2:1–7, 12; 1 CORINTHIANS 14:13–19, KJV

1 And when the day of Pentecost was fully come, they were all with one accord in one place.

2 And suddenly there came a sound from heaven as of a rushing mighty wind, and it filled all the house where they were sitting.

3 And there appeared unto them cloven tongues like as of fire, and it sat upon each of them.

4 And they were all filled with the Holy Ghost, and began to speak with other tongues, as the Spirit gave them utterance.

5 And there were dwelling at Jerusalem Jews, devout men, out of every nation under heaven.

6 Now when this was noised abroad, the multitude came together, and were confounded, because that every man heard them speak in his own language.

7 And they were all amazed and marvelled, saying one to another, Behold, are not all these which speak Galilaeans?

12 And they were all amazed, and were in doubt, saying one to another, What meaneth this?

14:13 Wherefore let him that speaketh in an unknown tongue pray that he may interpret.

14 For if I pray in an unknown tongue, my spirit prayeth, but my understanding is unfruitful.

15 What is it then? I will pray with the spirit, and I will pray with the understanding also: I will sing with the spirit, and I will sing with the understanding also.

16 Else when thou shalt bless with the spirit, how shall he that occupieth the room of the unlearned say Amen at thy giving of thanks, seeing he understandeth not what thou sayest?

17 For thou verily givest thanks well, but he other is not edified.

18 I thank my God, I speak with tongues more than ye all:

19 Yet in the church I had rather speak five words with my understanding, that by my voice I might teach others also, than ten thousand words in an unknown tongue.

BIBLICAL DEFINITIONS
A. Transgressions (Amos 2:4, 6) *pesha'* (Heb.)—Willful deviation from, and therefore rebellion against, the path of moral or godly living.
B. Despised (v. 4) *ma'as* (Heb.)—To reject, refuse, despise.

LIFE NEED FOR TODAY'S LESSON
AIM: Students will learn that communication is important as believers work together through worship, praise, and programs to build the church.

INTRODUCTION
Chaos in Communication
After the chapter on love, Paul turns to the place of tongues in the church gathering. Some had prided themselves on speaking in tongues. This led them to cause chaos in their gatherings. Those who were new to the church could not understand what was going on. Paul attempts to guide the Corinthian church in how to use the gift of tongues and what gifts they ought to be seeking. His main goal in the whole matter is that any contribution a member makes in the church would be strengthened and encouraged.

BIBLE LEARNING
AIM: Students will affirm the reality of spiritual gifts.

I. A CASE OF CLEAR COMMUNICATION (Acts 2:1–7, 12)
At the beginning of Acts, we see God's heart communicate clearly His salvation to all the nations. The apostles were told to wait in Jerusalem until they were empowered by the Holy Spirit. The sign of this was tongues of fire resting over their heads. We do not know whether these tongues actually consisted of real fire or were just a metaphor. Regardless, these tongues of fire were a symbol of the fact that the apostles were empowered to speak for the Lord. Immediately they began to praise God as "the Spirit gave utterance," and the crowd of Jewish pilgrims who had come from all over for the feast of Pentecost heard them speak in their own language (vv. 4–6).

The Outpouring of the Spirit (verses 1–7, 12)
1 And when the day of Pentecost was fully come, they were all with one accord in one place.

The narrative opens with a reference to the time and place of the coming of the Holy Spirit. The time is precise: "when the day of Pentecost was fully come." The word "Pentecost" (Gk. *pentekoste*, **pen-tay-kos-TAY**) literally means "fiftieth," because it was celebrated 50 days after Passover. It was the second of the three great Jewish annual festivals (**Deuteronomy 16:16**), falling between Passover and the Feast of Tabernacles, or Feast of Booths. Pentecost was also called the Feast of Weeks because it was held seven weeks after Passover (**Exodus 34:22**). It had a double meaning. Pentecost celebrated the end of the grain harvest and was also known as the Feast of Harvest (**Exodus 23:16**). In later Judaism (toward the 1st century A.D.), it was observed as the anniversary of the giving of the Law

LESSON 1 • JUNE 1, 2025

to Moses at Sinai. It is possible to draw out from the two meanings of Pentecost a double symbolism for Christians. The coming of the Holy Spirit occurred 50 days after the crucifixion and resurrection of Christ, marking the beginning of the new covenant and the harvesting of the firstfruits of the Christian missionary enterprise.

The Day of Pentecost "was fully come" (Gk. *sumpleroo*, **soom-play-RAH-oh**), which means that it was in the process of fulfillment or coming to an end.

The expression "in one place" probably refers to their usual meeting place somewhere within the temple area, such as one of the many rooms or halls of the temple (cf. **Acts 2:46; 3:11; 5:12**).

2 And suddenly there came a sound from heaven as of a rushing mighty wind, and it filled all the house where they were sitting.

The place where the disciples were gathered was suddenly filled with what sounded like "a rushing mighty wind" from heaven. The word "wind" (Gk. *pnoe*, **pno-AY**) is frequently used in the Bible as a symbol of the Spirit (**1 Kings 19:11; Ezekiel 37:9-14; John 3:8**). The Spirit came upon them with great power. This was the power promised by Jesus for witnessing (**Luke 24:49; Acts 1:8**).

3 And there appeared unto them cloven tongues like as of fire, and it sat upon each of them.

The disciples not only heard the sound of a rushing mighty wind, but they saw "tongues like as of fire." The word "fire" (Gk. *pur*, **poor**) also denotes the divine presence (**Exodus 3:2**) and the Spirit who purifies and sanctifies (cf. **Matthew 3:11; Luke 3:16**).

The expression "cloven tongues" (Gk. *diamerizo glossa*, **dee-ah-meh-REED-zo GLOH-sah**) refers to tongues dividing, distributing, or parting themselves. Then the tongues "sat" (Gk. *kathizo*, **kah-THEED-zo**) on the disciples. The verb is singular, giving the understanding that a tongue of fire sat on each person.

4 And they were all filled with the Holy Ghost, and began to speak with other tongues, as the Spirit gave them utterance.

The disciples were all filled with the Holy Spirit (cf. **Acts 4:8; 13:9; Ephesians 5:18**), and they "began to speak with other tongues." Speaking in tongues is also called glossolalia, from two Greek words: *glossa* (**GLOH-sah**), tongue, and *laleo* (**lah-LEH-oh**), to speak. It was not an unparalleled manifestation (cf. **Acts 10:46; 19:6**). It was also a spiritual gift that was highly valued by the church of Corinth (**1 Corinthians 12–14**). Without denying that it was a manifestation of the Holy Spirit, Paul denounced the undue importance that some people of the Corinthian church attached to it. The glossolalia in Corinth was uttered in speech that could not be understood until someone present received the corresponding spiritual gift of interpretation. Speaking in tongues is similar to the prophetic utterances of people possessed by the Spirit of God in the Old Testament (**Numbers 11:25–29; 1 Samuel 10:5–6**).

In **Acts 2**, however, the disciples were speaking in tongues that were completely different from their native languages, as prompted by the Holy Spirit. The words they were speaking were immediately recognized by immigrants and visitors from many parts of the world. The following verse (**v. 5**) shows that the purpose of the Spirit-inspired glossolalia was to symbolize the universality of the Gospel (**Acts 1:8**). It shows that people from all nations will be brought into a unity of understanding through the preaching of the Gospel in the power of the Holy Spirit.

LESSON 1 • JUNE 1, 2025

5 And there were dwelling at Jerusalem Jews, devout men, out of every nation under heaven.

The verb translated as "were dwelling" (Gk. *katoikeo*, **kat-oy-KEH-oh**) is used for temporary dwellers who came for Pentecost. They had come from "every nation under heaven" to stay in Jerusalem near the temple within the city walls as permanent residents. The expression "every nation under heaven" also stresses the international nature of the crowd. The crowd was composed of permanent residents of Jerusalem and visitors who had came to celebrate the feast.

6 Now when this was noised abroad, the multitude came together, and were confounded, because that every man heard them speak in his own language.

They "were confounded" (Gk. *suncheo*, **soonKHEH-oh**) as they heard loud praises to God uttered by the disciples in the indigenous languages and dialects of their native lands. The word "language" (Gk. *dialektos*, **dee-AH-lektoce**) means the language of a particular nation or region. It can refer to a whole language or even dialects within a language. The diversity of language is stressed here and in the following verses (**v. 7–12**). The desire of God is that every tribe and nation will be reached with the Gospel (cf. **1 Timothy 2:4–7; Revelation 5:9**).

7 And they were all amazed and marvelled, saying one to another, Behold, are not all these which speak Galilaeans?

They were "amazed" (Gk. *existemi*, **ex-IS-taymee**), which literally means to be beside oneself or out of place, denoting an overwhelming surprise. They "marvelled" (Gk. *thaumazo*, **thowMAHD-zo**), denoting a continuing wonder and speculation as they heard loud praises to God uttered in languages and dialects other than the speakers' native Galilaean. The Galilaeans used a peculiar dialect that distinguished them from other Judeans (cf. **Matthew 26:73; Mark 14:70**).

12 And they were all amazed, and were in doubt, saying one to another, What meaneth this?

Again we see that the visitors present on the Day of Pentecost are amazed. This verse also adds that they were in doubt (Gk. *diaporeo*, **dee-ah-poh-REH-oh**). This word means to be totally at a loss. They were at a loss for an explanation of the events they were experiencing. As a result, they ask themselves "What meaneth (Gk. *thelo*, **THEH-lo**) this?" Thelo can specifically mean to intend or to purpose. In essence, the travelers are asking, "What is the purpose of our being able to hear and see this phenomenon?"
ed to have this event interpreted for them.

II. THE CALL TO CLEAR COMMUNICATION (1 Corinthians 14:13–15)

Years later, in the Corinthian church, Paul discusses the need for clear communication. The church had been blessed with miraculous gifts, including the ability to speak in unknown tongues. From the text here and in **1 Corinthians 12**, we can see that this ability to speak in unknown tongues was different from what the apostles experienced at Pentecost. These were tongues that were not known and needed miraculous or supernatural interpretation (**1 Corinthians 12:10, 14:5, 27**). The Corinthians had placed a higher priority on speaking in tongues than other gifts that brought more clarity and built up the whole church. They were more interested in gifts that built up and elevated self.

Order for Speaking in Tongues (verses 13–15)

13 Wherefore let him that speaketh in an unknown tongue pray that he may interpret.

LESSON 1 • JUNE 1, 2025

The "wherefore" (Gk. *dio*, **dee-OH**) connects this sentence with Paul's preceding thoughts. Since those who earnestly desire spiritual gifts must seek to edify the church, then the one speaking in an unknown tongue must pray for God to give him or her the interpretation of what he or she is saying. The word for tongue here is glossa, the generic word for tongue or language. This is translated as "unknown" tongue because the one speaking it does not need to study a known foreign language to understand what is being said. Instead, the one speaking in a tongue is encouraged to pray or ask for divine help to interpret what he or she is saying.

14 For if I pray in an unknown tongue, my spirit prayeth, but my understanding is unfruitful. 15 What is it then? I will pray with the spirit, and I will pray with the understanding also: I will sing with the spirit, and I will sing with the understanding also.

Next Paul describes the dynamics of unknown tongues. When worshipers speak in unknown tongues, their spirit or inner self is praying. At the same time, they have not understood anything that they have said. The word "unfruitful" is *akarpos* (Gk. **AH-kar-poce**), and means to be barren or not yielding what it ought to yield. Paul is saying that speaking in tongues is unproductive as far as the mind's understanding is concerned. Paul then states his own approach to unknown tongues. He will pray "with the spirit," another way of saying praying in unknown tongues. This will be accompanied by praying with understanding as well. He also states that he will sing in unknown tongues, but with understanding.

QUESTION 1
What did Paul tell the Corinthians to pray for when they spoke in unknown tongues (**1 Corinthians 14:13**)?

III. THE CONVICTION FOR CLEAR COMMUNICATION (vv. 16–19)

Paul's point is that the gift of tongues is not worth anything unless it brings about clarity in communication. They can speak in unknown tongues in a public meeting, and it wouldn't help anyone but themselves.

Sharing for Understanding (verses 16–19)

16 Else when thou shalt bless with the spirit, how shall he that occupieth the room of the unlearned say Amen at thy giving of thanks, seeing he understandeth not what thou sayest? 17 For thou verily givest thanks well, but the other is not edified.

The results of speaking in unknown tongues are obvious. The one who is a novice or unlearned in the Christian faith (idiotes) will not be able to understand what is being said. Paul uses the word *eulogeo* (Gk. **ehoo-lohGEH-oh**), which means to speak well of someone or something. It is commonly translated as bless. Here he is saying that the person speaking in tongues is doing a good thing by speaking well of God, but at the same time, it is not good for the assembly or worship gathering when no one understands.

18 I thank my God, I speak with tongues more than ye all: 19 Yet in the church I had rather speak five words with my understanding, that by my voice I might teach others also, than ten thousand words in an unknown tongue.

Here we see that Paul participated in speaking in unknown tongues. In order to drive the point home to the Corinthian church, he boasts that he speaks in tongues more than all of them. Although this is the case, he would rather speak a small amount with understanding so that he can teach others, than ten thousand words in an unknown tongue which neither he nor his hearers could understand. The word for ten thousand (Gk. *murios*, MOOree-oce) was the largest number the Greek language of the time had. Paul uses this hyperbole to show just how much he desired communication in the church to be intelligible.

QUESTION 2
What is the goal of our communication in a church setting (**v. 17**)?

BIBLE APPLICATION
AIM: Students will participate with the church in recognizing and celebrating its founding on the day of Pentecost.

There are approximately 6,500 languages in the world, not counting unspoken languages or codes. There is also the particular dialect and slang of numerous subcultures. With all of these different languages, it is not hard to believe that we live in a world where people do not understand one another. As followers of Christ, we are called to bridge the language gap. Whether it is a spoken language or what some may call "Christianese," we are called to interpret and make clear what God wants to say to the world. If people cannot understand at first, it is our responsibility to relay God's message so that they can receive it.

STUDENTS' RESPONSES
AIM: Students will affirm the importance of mutual edification in church life.

We as Christians have our own theological and church language. This week, make a list of those words or phrases that would sound strange to those who have no understanding of the Christian faith. Write out ways that you can communicate these concepts to others who are not in the church without losing the meaning.

PRAYER
Dear Lord, help us to listen, appreciate, learn, and affirm one another. Let us be cautious and respectful of those who speak or listen through different cultural and language experiences. May we strive to work together in unity and love. In Jesus' Name we pray. Amen.

Digging Deeper
Gift of Languages
There is an important piece of background reading for a lesson like this. We should consult "The Doctrines of the Church of God in Christ" to review the Church's teaching about the Baptism of the Holy Ghost. (The Doctrines are reprinted, for our convenience, at the back of both the annual and the quarterly commentaries of the Sunday School lessons.) To quote: "We believe the baptism of the Holy Ghost is an experience subsequent to conversion and sanctification and that tongue-speaking is the consequence of the baptism in the Holy Ghost with the manifestation of the fruit of the spirit" (emphasis mine). As our founder Bishop C.H. Mason taught, Scripture demonstrates that spirit baptism is evidenced by speaking in tongues (Acts 2:4; Acts 10:44–46; Acts 19:1–6). To quote again from the Doctrine, "When one receives a baptismal Holy Ghost experience, we believe one will speak with a tongue unknown to oneself according to the sovereign will of Christ." In that sense, the initial experience of tongue-speaking for a believer is a sign that the believer is now filled with the Spirit.

However, the clear teaching of Scripture is that there is also a spiritual gift of tongues distributed to believers as the Holy Ghost sees fit. "Do all speak with tongues?" Paul asked, referring to the gift (1 Cor.12:30). The answer is "no" because the gift of tongues is not given to every believer (just

LESSON 1 • JUNE 1, 2025

as the gifts of the working of miracles and healing are not given to everyone). As my late Church Mother once said, "Every Saint will have spoken in tongues once, but some may never speak in tongues again."

HOW TO SAY IT

Galileans. ga-lih-**LEE**-ins.

Occupieth. ok-yu-**PIE**-ith.

PREPARE FOR NEXT SUNDAY

Read **Amos 2:4 — 8** and study "Judgment On Israel And Judah."

Sources:
Hays, Richard B. *First Corinthians: Interpretation, A Bible Commentary for Teaching and Preaching.* Louisville, KY: John Knox. 1997.
Henry, Matthew. *Matthew Henry's Commentary on the Whole Bible: Complete and Unabridged in One Volume.* Peabody, MA: Hendrickson, 1994.
Prime, Derek. *Opening Up 1 Corinthians.* Opening Up Commentary. Leominster, UK: Day One Publications, 2005.
Utley, Robert James. *Paul's Letters to a Troubled Church: I and II Corinthians.* Study Guide Commentary Series, vol. 6. Marshall, TX: Bible Lessons International, 2002.

DAILY HOME BIBLE READINGS

MONDAY
Made You Hear God's Voice
(Deuteronomy 4:32–40)

TUESDAY
A Small Member, Great Boasting
(James 3:1–5)

WEDNESDAY
All Languages, One Loud Voice
(Revelation 7:9–12)

THURSDAY
We Hear in Our Own Languages
(Acts 2:8–13)

FRIDAY
They Shall Prophesy
(Acts 2:14–21)

SATURDAY
Excel in Your Gifts
(1 Corinthians 14:6–12)

SUNDAY
Building Up Others
(Acts 2:1–7, 12;
1 Corinthians 14:13–19)

COMMENTS / NOTES:

LESSON 2 • JUNE 8, 2025

JUDGMENT ON ISRAEL AND JUDAH

BIBLE BASIS: AMOS 2:4-8

BIBLE TRUTH: God will not overlook injustice, but will punish the unjust.

MEMORY VERSE: "Thus saith the LORD; For three transgressions of Judah, and for four, I will not turn away the punishment thereof; because they have despised the law of the LORD, and have not kept his commandments, and their lies caused them to err, after the which their fathers have walked" (Amos 2:4).

LESSON AIM: By the end of the lesson, your students will: REVIEW God's judgment of Judah and Israel; ENCOURAGE sensitivity toward social injustice; and ADDRESS issues of injustice in their local and global communities.

BACKGROUND SCRIPTURE: Amos 2:4-8; Psalm 75—Read and incorporate the insights gained from the Background Scriptures into your study of the lesson.

LESSON SCRIPTURE

AMOS 2:4-8, KJV

4 Thus saith the LORD; For three transgressions of Judah, and for four, I will not turn away the punishment thereof; because they have despised the law of the LORD, and have not kept his commandments, and their lies caused them to err, after the which their fathers have walked:

5 But I will send a fire upon Judah, and it shall devour the palaces of Jerusalem.

6 Thus saith the LORD; For three transgressions of Israel, and for four, I will not turn away the punishment thereof; because they sold the righteous for silver, and the poor for a pair of shoes;

7 That pant after the dust of the earth on the head of the poor, and turn aside the way of the meek: and a man and his father will go in unto the same maid, to profane my holy name:

8 And they lay themselves down upon clothes laid to pledge by every altar, and they drink the wine of the condemned in the house of their god.

BIBLICAL DEFINITIONS

A. Transgressions (Amos 2:4, 6) *pesha'* (Heb.)—Willful deviation from, and therefore rebellion against, the path of moral or godly living.

B. Despised (v. 4) *ma'as* (Heb.)—To reject, refuse, despise.

LIFE NEED FOR TODAY'S LESSON

AIM: Students will know that even though people know right from wrong, some people treat others unjustly.

INTRODUCTION
The Prophet Amos

The prophet Amos was born in the city of Tekoa. He prophesied in Israel around 750 B.C. He was not the descendant of prophets; rather he was from "among the herdsman of Tekoa" (**Amos 1:1**). He was a shepherd and also tended and gathered sycamore figs. He received his call to ministry while he was out in the pastures, with his sheep (**Amos 7:14-15**). His career as a shepherd and a common working man informed his

LESSON 2 • JUNE 8, 2025

view of the world and the way he communicated his prophetic message. He used images from nature and agriculture in his prophecies. Amos lived during an era of relative peace and prosperity. This prosperity led to an atmosphere of indulgent luxury, corrupt power, and moral depravity in Israel. Many had turned to the worship of idols and other gods. Some religious practices were still maintained; however, these had deteriorated into empty rituals. Israel's religion didn't have the intended impact on how they lived their lives.

BIBLE LEARNING
AIM: Students will learn that God hates injustice and oppression of the poor.

I. Judah's Sin and God's Judgment (Amos 2:4–5)

Amos delivers his message from the Lord, explaining the sins that Judah has committed. Judah's sin is repetitive; a continual pattern of disobedience. Their sins are numerous and God's patience with Judah has run out. In this regard, Judah is no different than the other nations that God has judged. The same pattern, "for three transgressions ... and for four" used to judge pagan nations, is used here as well. However, Judah's sin is different in that they had received God's laws and chosen not to follow them. Rather than keeping His laws, they have "despised the Law of the LORD." The word translated "despised" in the KJV is the Hebrew word *ma'as* (**mah-AHS**), also meaning to reject or refuse. Judah knew what to do, but refused to do it.

Judah's Judgment and Punishment (verses 4–5)

4 Thus saith the LORD; For three transgressions of Judah and for four, I will not turn away the punishment thereof; because they have despised the law of the LORD, and have not kept his commandments, and their lies caused them to err, after which their fathers have walked.

By moving from neighboring nations on to Judah, Amos begins to zero in on the goal of prophesying against Israel. Judah is condemned for rejecting the Law of God and for idolatry. Although the actual word "idolatry" is not mentioned, we can infer this from the reference to lies (Heb. *kazab*, **kah-ZAHV**) making them err. The word "lies" is often used in reference to idols or anything that gives them false hope (**Psalm 4:2; Ezekiel 13:6**). The idols of the nations only lead people into deception. The sin of idolatry is also alluded to with the phrase "after which their fathers have walked." "Walking after" is often used in reference to idol worship or following the commands and statutes of Yahweh (**Deuteronomy 8:19; Jeremiah 8:2**). It is obvious Amos is referring to the former since he has already stated that Judah has "despised" (Heb. *ma'as*, **mahAHS**) God's Law.

This oracle against Judah stands out from the prophetic oracles against the other nations because Judah is closest to Israel and Judah's sins are of a covenantal nature, not just crimes against humanity. They are indicted for their breach of covenant with God by going after idols. This is something that God does not take lightly with His covenant people.

5 But I will send a fire upon Judah, and it shall devour the palaces of Jerusalem.

Amos announces that Judah's sins will not go unpunished. The Lord will send a fire on Judah and the palaces (Heb. *'armon*, **ar-MONE**) of Jerusalem. Most likely, Amos is referring to the citadels and strongholds that made up the king's palace and temple complex, since this word for "palace" can also mean citadel or fortress. The word comes from a root meaning high and lofty. These high and lofty places would be brought down by fire. This

LESSON 2 • JUNE 8, 2025

happened in 586 B.C. when Nebuchadnezzar and the Babylonian army defeated Jerusalem through siege.

QUESTION 1
What conditions do you think contributed to Judah's rejection of God's Law and reliance on the false teaching of their ancestors (**Amos 2:4**)?

II. ISRAEL'S SIN (vv. 6–8)

Amos completes his message with a stern rebuke of Israel. Israel's spiritual climate has fallen to the point that they resemble the foreign nations around them. Their sin and rejection of God's Law places them squarely in the company of nations that haven't even received it. Again, the prophecy indicates an identical pattern of judgement: "For three transgressions … and for four."

The innocent and the poor are being abused in Israel. Though slavery is a customary practice, Amos speaks to the rigged and unjust practice of driving debtors to slavery for the sole purpose of benefiting the powerful and wealthy. Rather than being merciful and allowing them more time to repay, people are driven into slavery. For as little as the cost of a pair of sandals, the poor and innocent are dealt with harshly. Additionally, those sold into slavery are abused within the households of the wealthy. A man and his son lying with the same servant woman is a violation of Moses' Law and profanes God's name (**Exodus 20:17**). A servant given in marriage to a son is to be treated as a daughter by the master of the house (**Exodus 21:9**).

Injustice and Pain (verses 6–8)

6 Thus saith the LORD; For three transgressions of Israel, and for four, I will not turn away the punishment thereof; because they sold the righteous for silver, and the poor for a pair of shoes.

Now Amos turns his prophetic gaze toward Israel. As Amos prophesied against the other nations like Tyre, Edom, Moab, and Judah, Israel must have savored and enjoyed hearing their neighbors' condemnation. Now it was their turn. The Lord would not be partial but would judge fairly. If the other nations received prophetic pronouncements of judgment, then Israel would receive judgment as well.

Amos repeats the same prophetic formula "for three transgressions of Israel and for four." This was an acknowledgment of God's patience toward their sin. Adding "for four" showed that God was at His limit and could not restrain His punishment for their wrongdoing. This wrongdoing manifested itself in selling "the righteous for silver, and the poor for a pair of shoes." The word "righteous" (Heb. *tsaddiyq*, **tsah-DEEK**) here may be used in a legal sense, referencing those who are innocent in Israel's law courts but who nevertheless are found guilty by corrupt judges. It could also be referring to those sold into slavery for a debt. Both meanings could be in view here. A pair of sandals could be referring to land transfer (see **Ruth 4**) or a very small, insignificant debt. Amos was pointing out how the Israelites were devaluing human life.

7 That pant after the dust of the earth on the head of the poor, and turn aside the way of the meek: and a man and his father will go in unto the same maid, to profane my holy name.

Israel is accused of having little or no regard for the poor. The word "pant" (Heb. *sha'ap*, **shah-AHF**) is often rendered "swallow up" or "trample." They trample the head of the poor into the earth, meaning they provide no means for the poor to better themselves. Instead, Israel is accused of wanting the poor to remain poor for their own benefit and personal gain.

LESSON 2 • JUNE 8, 2025

They also push the meek or afflicted out of the way and do not give alms or financial, social, or physical assistance.

Their social evils extend into the realm of sexual immorality as well. The sexual sin presented breaches proper familial relationship and is condemned (**Leviticus 18:15, 20:12**). The word used for girl (Heb. *na'arah*, **nah-ah-RAH**) can also be rendered female servant. For both father and son to have sexual relations with the same slave girl would be a misuse of power by exploiting those who have no rights to speak up for themselves. This abuse of power made their acts an even greater violation of God's covenant. Such acts profane, defile, or stain the Lord's holy name. The Hebrew word *chalal* (**khih-LEL**) expresses the hideous act of desecrating that which belongs to God. It is making unholy that which is deemed holy. The Israelites are particularly accused of defiling the Lord's name through sexual and social sins.

8 And they lay themselves down upon clothes laid to pledge by every altar, and they drink the wine of the condemned in the house of their god.

Amos continues to show how Israel has sinned. They are accused of "laying themselves down upon clothes laid to pledge by every altar." Their sexual immorality and injustice (**v. 7**) was connected to their religious sin and unfaithfulness to their covenant with God. Part of their idolatrous practices was to worship through sexual acts. Their crime is even more serious, as they commit these acts on clothes that have been taken as collateral for a loan. The law stated that these garments (usually the outer garments or cloaks) were to be returned for the night (**Exodus 22:26**). Instead they were kept to be used for shameful acts. The perpetrators also drank wine, which was paid for by "unjust fines" (NLT). It is not clear whether these fines are unjust taxes or part of the tithe to the "house of their god."

During this time, ancient Israel had set up shrines and temples to replace the temple of Yahweh at Jerusalem. At these shrines, Yahweh was represented as a bull, which was also the representation of Baal. It is not surprising that because of this syncretistic mix of ideas, their worship was also patterned after the worship of Baal to include orgiastic rituals.

QUESTION 2

The poor are sold into slavery for what amounted to the cost of a pair of sandals. Do you think greed motivated the actions of the wealthy? What other evil rationale may have driven their actions (**v. 6**)?

BIBLE APPLICATION

AIM: Students will know they are called to stand for justice even though this may necessitate standing against others.

The powerful and wealthy in Israel used legitimate political and legal systems to enrich themselves and hold down the less fortunate. A parallel to this type of behavior is the modernday practice of predatory lending in America. Predatory lending occurs when wealthy banking institutions provide loans under terms that are misleading or abusive. Often the loan terms make it impossible for a borrower to repay the loan or make the required payments. This results in the debtor losing land, money, or property to the bank. The poor and less educated are often the primary targets of such lending practices. Rather than taking advantage of the less fortunate, God calls us to minister to those that need help (**Matthew 25:34–35**).

STUDENTS' RESPONSES

AIM: Students will discuss how Christians are involved in corporate injustices.

As a nation and as the church, when it comes to social injustice, we often point the finger at others. Prayerfully make a list of the ways our nation and the church contribute to social injustice. Commit to practicing justice in these areas of life as an individual.

PRAYER

God of justice, we are sorry for any injustices that we have actively or unknowingly committed in our lives. We seek justice for all and thank You for allowing Your justice to prevail in us. In Jesus' Name we pray. Amen.

Digging Deeper
Three…Four

Throughout Amos 1-2, there is a pattern to the words of the prophet, *For three transgressions of … and for four, I will not turn away the punishment thereof …* (Amos 1:3, 6, 9, 11, 13; 2:14, 6). Remember that Amos is a prophet from the Southern kingdom whom God calls to prophesy to the Northern kingdom (Amos 7:10-12). When the readers put themselves into the shoes of the original hearers of the prophetic message, you can hear them agreeing with the pronounced impending judgments on the foreign nations, including Judah. But when the proverbial finger is pointed at Israel, the tone changes. The indictment is longer, and the judgment is assured.

Amos' use of the rhetorical device, *"For three transgressions … and four …"* highlights the completeness of the coming judgment. This same pattern of giving a number and then adding one is also seen in the Proverbs (cf. Job 5:18–9 33:14; Prov 6:16-19).

Three things are never satisfied; four never say, "Enough" … (Proverbs 30:15-17).

Three things are too wonderful for me, four I do not understand … (Proverbs 30:18-19).

Under three things the earth trembles; under four it cannot bear up … (Proverbs 30:21-23).

It's interesting to note that while the Proverbs list four items, Amos identifies only one. It's almost as if the list of transgressions (Hebrew: *pesha*) is so long that God chooses to identify only one, that is until he gets to the charges against Israel.

HOW TO SAY IT

Devour. Di-**VOW**-er.

Profane. pro-**FAYN**.

DAILY HOME BIBLE READINGS

MONDAY
I Will Judge with Equity
(Psalm 75)

TUESDAY
I Will Press You Down
(Amos 2:9–16)

WEDNESDAY
I Will Punish Your Iniquities
(Amos 3:1–8)

THURSDAY
I Will Punish Your Transgressions
(Amos 3:9–15)

FRIDAY
Judgment is Surely Coming
(Amos 4:1–6)

SATURDAY
You Did Not Return to Me
(Amos 4:7–13)

SUNDAY
I Will Not Revoke Punishment
(Amos 2:4–8)

PREPARE FOR NEXT SUNDAY

Read **Amos 5:14–15, 18–27** and study "God is Not Fooled."

Sources:
Alexander, David and Pat Alexander. *Zondervan Handbook to the Bible.* Grand Rapids, MI: Zondervan, 1999. 490.
Burge, Gary M. and Andrew E. Hill, eds. *Baker Illustrated Bible Commentary.* Grand Rapids, MI: Baker Books, 2012. 834.

LESSON 2 • JUNE 8, 2025

Butler, Trent C., ed. *Holman Bible Dictionary*. Electronic Edition, Quickverse. Nashville, TN: Holman Bible Publishers, 1991. S.vv. "Amos," "Slavery in the Old Testament," and "Tekoa."

Carson, D. A., R. T. France, J. A. Motyer, and G. J. Wenham, eds. *New Bible Commentary*. Downer's Grove, IL: InterVarsity Press, 1994. 796–797.

Easton, M. G. *Easton's Bible Dictionary*. 1st ed. Oklahoma City: Ellis Enterprises, 1993. S.vv. "Amos," "Slave," and "Tekoa."

Motyer, J. A. The Message of Amos. Downers Grove, IL: InterVarsity Press, 1974. 49–60.

Orr, James, ed. "Tekoa." *International Standard Bible Encyclopedia*. Electronic Edition. Omaha, NE: Quickverse, 1998.

Strong, James. *The New Strong's Exhaustive Concordance Of The Bible Expanded Edition*. Nashville, TN: Thomas Nelson, 2001. S.vv. "Ma'ac" and "Pasha."

Stuart, Douglas. *Word Biblical Commentary: Hosea–Jonah*. Nashville, TN: Thomas Nelson, 1987. 304–305, 315–318.

Walton, John H., Victor H. Matthews, and Mark W. Chavalas. *The IVP Bible Background Commentary: Old Testament*. Downers Grove, IL: InterVarsity Press, 2000. 764.

COMMENTS / NOTES:

LESSON 3 • JUNE 15, 2025

GOD IS NOT FOOLED

BIBLE BASIS: AMOS 5:14–15, 18–27

BIBLE TRUTH: Amos declared to the people that God will not be fooled by insincere offerings and will severely punish all sinners.

MEMORY VERSE: "But let judgment run down as waters, and righteousness as a mighty stream" (Amos 5:24).

LESSON AIM: By the end of the lesson, your students will: KNOW how God establishes justice for the righteous and punishes deceivers; RECOGNIZE and reflect on actions of injustice within the community of faith; and IDENTIFY unjust practices, commit to stop our participation in them, and help others do the same.

BACKGROUND SCRIPTURE: Amos 5; Hosea 11:1–7—Read and incorporate the insights gained from the Background Scriptures into your study of the lesson.

LESSON SCRIPTURE

AMOS 5:14–15, 18–27, KJV

14 Seek good, and not evil, that ye may live: and so the LORD, the God of hosts, shall be with you, as ye have spoken.

15 Hate the evil, and love the good, and establish judgment in the gate: it may be that the LORD God of hosts will be gracious unto the remnant of Joseph.

18 Woe unto you that desire the day of the LORD! to what end is it for you? the day of the LORD is darkness, and not light.

19 As if a man did flee from a lion, and a bear met him; or went into the house, and leaned his hand on the wall, and a serpent bit him.

20 Shall not the day of the LORD be darkness, and not light? even very dark, and no brightness in it?

21 I hate, I despise your feast days, and I will not smell in your solemn assemblies.

22 Though ye offer me burnt offerings and your meat offerings, I will not accept them: neither will I regard the peace offerings of your fat beasts.

23 Take thou away from me the noise of thy songs; for I will not hear the melody of thy viols.

24 But let judgment run down as waters, and righteousness as a mighty stream.

25 Have ye offered unto me sacrifices and offerings in the wilderness forty years, O house of Israel?

26 But ye have borne the tabernacle of your Moloch and Chiun your images, the star of your god, which ye made to yourselves.

27 Therefore will I cause you to go into captivity beyond Damascus, saith the LORD, whose name is The God of hosts.

BIBLICAL DEFINITIONS

A. Gracious (Amos 5:15) *khanan* (Heb.)—To bend or stoop in kindness to an inferior; to be considerate; to show favor.

LESSON 3 • JUNE 15, 2025

B. Righteousness (v. 24) *tsedaqah* (Heb.)—Being in the right, justified, just.

LIFE NEED FOR TODAY'S LESSON
AIM: Students will know some people cover their evil ways with outward acts of goodness.

INTRODUCTION
The Death of Israel
Amos begins **chapter 5** as a eulogy for the "dead" nation of Israel. Israel isn't yet dead, but the lament is meant to impress on the nation the severe danger it is in. The death of Israel is described as the death of a virgin (**Amos 5:2**). The death of a virgin would have been considered particularly tragic because she had no children to carry on her memory. This type of death is distinctly permanent. Furthermore, the dead virgin is described as having been left lying in a field, unburied. To leave a body unburied would have been a shocking and appalling image to consider, yet this is how the demise of Israel is described. Its depraved moral climate and refusal to turn back to God have indeed set it on the path of destruction.

BIBLE LEARNING
AIM: Students will reflect on how Judah and Israel's expression of faith was inconsistent with the ways they treated others and is a reminder of how our faith should be aligned with God's justice.

I. LOVE GOOD, HATE EVIL
(Amos 5:14–15)

Israel has become complacent in their presumption of God's favor (**v. 14**). Israel has mistakenly believed that, despite their sinful ways and their worship of other gods, they can still count on God's protection. However, Amos has declared to them that their actions have displeased God and will result in the destruction of their nation.

Choose Good Over Evil (verses 14–15)

14 Seek good, and not evil, that ye may live: and so the LORD, the God of hosts, shall be with you, as ye have spoken.

Amos continues with the refrain of seeking. The word seek (Heb. *darash*, **dah-RASH**) is used in **5:4** and **5:6** to refer to the people seeking the idol sanctuaries and then to refer to seeking God. Now Amos uses it in reference to good as opposed to evil. The good that the people were to seek was justice for the poor. Amos holds out the promise of the Lord's presence if they seek good. This highlights the fact that the Lord is not with them to begin with because of their injustice and oppression.

15 Hate the evil, and love the good, and establish judgment in the gate: it may be that the LORD God of hosts will be gracious unto the remnant of Joseph.

This seeking of good is more than just an outward action. It must radiate from an attitude of the heart. Amos uses strong words here. Seeking good is spelled out as hating (Heb. *sane'*, **sah-NAY**) evil. In other passages of the Old Testament, this word is used to refer to an enemy. The Israelites had been friends with evil and stood on the side of injustice. By using this word, Amos confronts them and challenges them to choose sides. Being on the side of good means establishing "judgment in the gate." The gates of the town were often used for courts of justice and centers of trade, and there the Israelites did most of their oppression of the poor. So this is where they could show that they loved good and hated evil instead.

If the people would seek Him and seek good instead of seeking the sanctuaries at Bethel

LESSON 3 • JUNE 15, 2025

and Gilgal, then maybe he would be gracious (Heb. *chanan*, **khah-NAHN**) to them. Amos is communicating that there is still the possibility of God showing favor and mercy to them. A remnant of Joseph is offered grace. After breaking away from the Southern Kingdom of Judah, the ten tribes were often referred to as Joseph. To refer to the remnant of Joseph is to appeal to those who will choose to seek good, although most of Israel will not.

QUESTION 1

What do you think it would have looked like for an Israelite to love good and hate evil during this time in Israel's history (**Amos 5:14–15**)?

II. A DAY OF DARKNESS (vv. 18–20)

Again, the prophet's message seizes on Israel's presumption of God's favor. It was common in times of trouble for the Israelites to long for "the day of the Lord," when God would rescue them from their enemies. But "the day of the Lord" will now be a day of reckoning.

God's Holy War Against Israel (verses 18–20)

18 Woe unto you that desire the day of the LORD! to what end is it for you? the day of the LORD is darkness, and not light. 19 As if a man did flee from a lion, and a bear met him; or went into the house, and leaned his hand on the wall, and a serpent bit him. 20 Shall not the day of the LORD be darkness, and not light? even very dark, and no brightness in it?

"The day of the Lord" is a term that refers to the Lord appearing and waging a holy war with His enemies. This is the first reference to the Day of the Lord in the Old Testament. Amos implies that those Israelites who were involved in oppressing the poor longed for this Day of Judgment. He lets them know that it will not be a good time for them; it will be darkness and not light. The images of running from a lion only to meet a bear or running into a house only to be bitten by a serpent describe the Day of the Lord as a time where they will not be able to escape God's judgment.

III. GOD DESIRES JUSTICE, NOT EMPTY RITUALS (vv. 21–24)

The worship of other gods had seeped into Israel's religious practices, but the people still maintained their Israelite rituals and festivals too. However, God is not fooled by their empty worship. True worship flows out of the hearts of those who earnestly seek to follow God's will. A true worshiper's relationships and personal life will be consistent with their public worship.

Israel's Despicable Acts (verses 21–24)

21 I hate, I despise your feast days, and I will not smell in your solemn assemblies. 22 Though ye offer me burnt offerings and your meat offerings, I will not accept them: neither will I regard the peace offerings of your fat beasts.

Outwardly impressive religious acts of good will that are selfishly done do not move the heart of God. The phrase "your feast days" (Heb. *chag*, **KHAG**) refers to the three main festivals that God established in Israel: Passover, Pentecost, and the Feast of Tabernacles (**Exodus 23:14–19; Deuteronomy 16:16–17**). Israel was abusing all of these festivals at this time. God rejected what Israel did in these feasts, which had a form of godliness but lacked the power thereof. The implication is that God Himself may establish events, activities, or procedures, but His people can pervert, abuse, and misuse them to achieve their own selfish ends. The Lord says He will not smell in their assemblies (Heb. *atsarah*,

LESSON 3 • JUNE 15, 2025

at-sa-RAH). Amos is possibly referring to the solemn assembly on the seventh day of Feast of Unleavened Bread and the eighth day of the Feast of Tabernacles (**Leviticus 23:8, 36**). The Lord would not be pleased with any of the worship practiced on those days because of the absence of justice and right living.

None of the offerings prescribed in the law would please God. The Lord would not accept their burnt offerings (Heb. *'olah*, **oh-LAH**), in which the whole animal was consumed with fire. This was a symbol of the total commitment of the worshiper's life to God. He would not accept their meat offerings (Heb. *minchah*, **min-KHAH**). These were sacrifices devoid of blood and intended as gifts to the Lord. Lastly, He would not accept their peace offerings (Heb. *shelem*, **SHEH-lem**), as these gifts were a sign of reconciliation or friendship, and this was not the state of their relationship with God. All of the worship rituals here were to be symbols of the people's real-life walk with the Lord, and offering them without the true reality behind them was hypocritical. This made their offerings unacceptable to the Lord.

23 Take thou away from me the noise of thy songs; for I will not hear the melody of thy viols.

Celebrations and rejoicing in God's presence played an important part in Israel's temple worship, which God had established. The Israelites used many kinds of musical instruments to praise God for His goodness and faithfulness (**2 Chronicles 7; Psalm 149**). In this instance the Lord actually calls their songs noise (Heb. *hamon*, **hah-MONE**). It is not the joyful noise of Psalm 100:1, but the noise and confusion of a host of people—noise that the Lord does not want to hear.

24 But let judgment run down as waters, and righteousness as a mighty stream.

God illustrates the nature of judgment (justice) and righteousness by using the phrases "run down as water" and "as a mighty stream," which speak of the ongoing and unobstructed movement of an ever-flowing body of water. The word for stream, *nakhal* (Heb. **NAH-khal**), is the word for the desert wadi. These small narrow valleys laid dry and barren for much of the year until a torrent of rain flooded them and made them into flowing streams. The Lord has already laid out the stipulations of justice in His covenant, and He is waiting for His people to fill the dry and barren land with justice and righteousness as the rains fill up a desert wadi.

QUESTION 2

What were the attitudes and motives of the Israelite worshipers (**vv. 21–23**)? Why did God refuse their worship?

IV. ISRAEL'S IDOLATRY RESULTS IN EXILE (vv. 25–27)

Israel's unfaithfulness is called out here. In addition to making offerings to Yahweh, they have begun worshiping foreign deities. Idol worship often included parades in which the people would carry handmade representations of their gods.

Judgment Against Hypocritical Worship (verses 25–27)

25 Have ye offered unto me sacrifices and offerings in the wilderness forty years, O house of Israel? 26 But ye have borne the tabernacle of your Moloch and Chiun your images, the star of your god, which ye made to yourselves. 27 Therefore will I cause you to go into captivity beyond Damascus, saith the LORD, whose name is The God of hosts.

The Lord ends His pronouncement of judgment upon Israel's hypocritical worship with a rhetorical question. He asks if the Israelites have offered sacrifices to Him in the wilderness. While there were sacrifices made to the Lord in the wilderness, they were not a regular feature in Israel's religious life until after the conquest. The Lord is affirming that His relationship with them was not dependent on sacrifices and offerings. He had been with them in the wilderness without regular sacrifices.

Next He confronts them on their worship of idols. They have paraded images of Sikkuth and Kaiwan through their streets to their shrines. Sacrifices, sacred dancing, and other perverse forms of worship followed this parade. Many translations say the "tabernacle of Moloch and Chiun your images." Other translations say "Sikkuth your king and Kaiwan your star god." The second translation is more probable as Sikkuth and Kaiwan were worshiped as astral deities in Mesopotamia connected to the planet Saturn. In ancient times, Saturn was observed as being a star and influencing agriculture. This explains the reference to "the star of your god" (**v. 26**). In the next verse, Amos predicts that instead of them carrying their gods to the shrine to worship, they will be carried away captive. The phrase "beyond Damascus" points toward the coming Assyrian invasion that would take place, and the resulting demise of the Northern Kingdom.

BIBLE APPLICATION

AIM: Students will discover that acting for justice requires putting aside self-interest.

Most Christians have no problem determining the difference between good and evil. In fact, even non-believers often choose to do the right thing. But merely choosing not to do evil is different than actively opposing evil. Opposing evil requires a level of conviction that goes beyond a simple understanding of right and wrong. It is often the case that only certain individuals will go out of their way to oppose an injustice. Most people are content to sit by while others are treated unfairly. It is God's desire that Christians would not only seek to do good, but also oppose evil and injustice. We are charged with standing for justice in our communities and in our world.

STUDENTS' RESPONSES

AIM: Students will listen to God's calls for justice and respond with a commitment to do justice.

It is often difficult in the moment to choose to love good and hate evil. One way to be prepared for those times and situations where we have decisions to make is to determine what is good or evil. Get a piece of paper and on one side write "Love Good" and on the other side write "Hate Evil." On the "Love Good" side, write all the ways that you can seek good in your daily life. On the "Hate Evil" side, write all the ways that you can hate evil in your daily life. Thinking about these things beforehand can help us to not only avoid falling into sin, but also move us forward in serving others in our community.

PRAYER

Lord, we worship You in spirit and in truth. May Your majestic and awesome power continue to give us the courage and strength that we need to choose good over evil. In Jesus' Name we pray. Amen.

DIGGING DEEPER

Whoa, Another Woe – On the Meaning of the Woe Sayings in Amos and the Prophets

Prophets use several forms of speech to communicate their message to God's people (for example, parables, laments, lawsuits, songs, et al.). One common form of communication

LESSON 3 • JUNE 15, 2025

was the "woe" (Ezekiel 18:18). "Woe" (Hebrew: *hoy*) was the word ancient Israelites cried out when facing disaster or death or when they mourned at a funeral.

For example, in Habakkuk 2, "woe" is pronounced four times by the Babylonians because they attack the people of God.
- *Woe to him who heaps up what is not his own* (v. 6b).
- *Woe to him who gets evil gain for his house* (v. 9a).
- *Woe to him who builds a town with blood and found a city on iniquity* (v. 12).
- *Woe to him who makes his neighbor drink … to gaze at their nakedness* (v. 15a).

By using the word "woe," God makes predictions of imminent doom. So, following the "woe" is the declaration for the "woe" and then the impending judgment. For example, Micah pronounces a woe" on those who devise wickedness and work evil on their beds, etc. (vv. 1-2). Therefore, God will bring disaster upon them (vv. 3-5).

HOW TO SAY IT
Tabernacle.   TA-ber-na-hul.

Damascus.   da-MAS-kus.

DAILY HOME BIBLE READINGS

MONDAY
Fools Say, "There is No God"
(Psalm 14)

TUESDAY
Can You Deceive God?
(Job 13:7–12)

WEDNESDAY
Full of Hypocrisy and Lawlessness
(Matthew 23:23–28)

THURSDAY
To Obey is Better than Sacrifice
(1 Samuel 15:7–23)

FRIDAY
I Know Your Transgressions and Sins
(Amos 5:7–13)

SATURDAY
Seek the Lord and Live
(Amos 5:1–6)

SUNDAY
Love Good and Establish Justice
(Amos 5:14–15, 18–27)

PREPARE FOR NEXT SUNDAY
Read **Amos 6:4–8, 11–14** and study "Rebuked for Selfishness."

Sources:
Alexander, David, and Pat Alexander. *Zondervan Handbook to the Bible*. Grand Rapids, MI: Zondervan, 1999. 490.
Burge, Gary M., and Andrew E. Hill, eds. *Baker Illustrated Bible Commentary*. Grand Rapids, MI: Baker Books, 2012. 834–835, 837–838.
Butler, Trent C., ed. *Holman Bible Dictionary*. Electronic Edition, Quickverse. Nashville, TN: Holman Bible Publishers, 1991. S.vv. "Kaiwan" and
"Prophet."
Easton, M. G. "Chiun." *Easton's Bible Dictionary*. 1st ed. Oklahoma City: Ellis Enterprises, 1993.
Kaiser, Walter C., and Duane Garrett, eds. "Prophets in the Bible and Pagan Nations." *Archaeological Study Bible*. Grand Rapids, MI: Zondervan, 2005.
Keck, Leander, ed. *The Twelve Prophets*. The New Interpreter's Bible. Vol. 7. Nashville, TN: Abingdon Press, 1996. 384–397.
Orr, James, ed. "Chiun." *International Standard Bible Encyclopedia*. Electronic Edition. Omaha, NE: Quickverse, 1998.

Strong, James. *The New Strong's Exhaustive Concordance Of The Bible Expanded Edition.* Nashville, TN: Thomas Nelson, 2001. S.vv. "Chanan" and "Tsadaqah."

Stuart, Douglas. *Word Biblical Commentary: Hosea–Jonah.* Nashville, TN: Thomas Nelson, 1987. 340–356.

Walton, John H., Victor H. Matthews, and Mark W. Chavalas. *The IVP Bible Background Commentary: Old Testament.* Downers Grove, IL: InterVarsity Press, 2000. 769–771.

COMMENTS / NOTES:

LESSON 4 • JUNE 22, 2025

REBUKED FOR SELFISHNESS

BIBLE BASIS: AMOS 6:4–8, 11–14

BIBLE TRUTH: God will dispossess the greedy and selfish and thus demonstrate God's justice.

MEMORY VERSE: "Shall horses run upon the rock? will one plow there with oxen? for ye have turned judgment into gall, and the fruit of righteousness into hemlock" (Amos 6:12).

LESSON AIM: By the end of the lesson, your students will: EXPLORE God's response to injustice as recorded by Amos; REFLECT on ways people practice greed and selfishness; and UNCOVER and DISCOVER ways God does justice amid injustice and ways humans can join God in the fight against injustice.

BACKGROUND SCRIPTURE: Amos 6; Psalm 119:31–38—Read and incorporate the insights gained from the Background Scriptures into your study of the lesson.

LESSON SCRIPTURE

AMOS 6:4–8, 11–14, KJV

4 That lie upon beds of ivory, and stretch themselves upon their couches, and eat the lambs out of the flock, and the calves out of the midst of the stall;

5 That chant to the sound of the viol, and invent to themselves instruments of musick, like David;

6 That drink wine in bowls, and anoint themselves with the chief ointments: but they are not grieved for the affliction of Joseph.

7 Therefore now shall they go captive with the first that go captive, and the banquet of them that stretched themselves shall be removed.

8 The Lord GOD hath sworn by himself, saith the LORD the God of hosts, I abhor the excellency of Jacob, and hate his palaces: therefore will I deliver up the city with all that is therein.

11 For, behold, the LORD commandeth, and he will smite the great house with breaches, and the little house with clefts.

12 Shall horses run upon the rock? will one plow there with oxen? for ye have turned judgment into gall, and the fruit of righteousness into hemlock:

13 Ye which rejoice in a thing of nought, which say, Have we not taken to us horns by our own strength?

14 But, behold, I will raise up against you a nation, O house of Israel, saith the LORD the God of hosts; and they shall afflict you from the entering in of Hemath unto the river of the wilderness.

BIBLICAL DEFINITIONS

A. Chant (Amos 6:5) *parat* (Heb.)—To improvise carelessly; to stammer.

B. Afflict (v. 14) *lakhats* (Heb.)—To squeeze or oppress.

LIFE NEED FOR TODAY'S LESSON

AIM: Students will discuss that some people care only about accumulating lavish possessions for themselves and care nothing for those who possess little.

LESSON 4 • JUNE 22, 2025

INTRODUCTION
Warning of Judgment

Amos proclaims prophecies from God that convict leaders for a lack of social justice and warning them of the "day of the Lord" when judgment would come to Israel. He has opposed the nation's sins and has encouraged them to repent for their evil and unjust ways. However, Israel has refused to turn away from their wickedness and remember the God they worshiped when they were in bondage. They are at risk for God's divine punishment.

BIBLE LEARNING
AIM: Students will affirm that true prosperity comes through obedience to God's commands.

I. A SELFISH LIFESTYLE (Amos 6:4–8)

The rich leaders of Samaria had completely turned all of their attention to their material wealth. They had become consumed with a lifestyle that was rich, elegant, exquisite, lavish, and excessive. They were only concerned with a higher standard of living that required the finest and best. From dining selections, fine clothing, wild parties, extravagant celebrations, grand mansions and expensive skin creams, the influential people of Israel had grown accustomed to a lifestyle that only served an elite class. Their lifestyle had caused them to lose focus on real-life issues around them. They were blind to the fact that as the elite became richer, the poor became poorer.

Loving Things Instead of God (verses 4–8)

4 That lie upon beds of ivory, and stretch themselves upon their couches, and eat the lambs out of the flock, and the calves out of the midst of the stall; 5 That chant to the sound of the viol, and invent to themselves instruments of musick, like David; 6 That drink wine in bowls, and anoint themselves with the chief ointments: but they are not grieved for the affliction of Joseph.

Verse 4 continues the woe that was declared in **verse 1**. In essence, he is saying, "Woe to you who put far off the day of doom . . . who sing idly to the sound of stringed instruments . . . who drink wine from bowls . . . but are not grieved." Amos had earlier prophesied against the houses of ivory, and now, it was the beds overlaid with ivory that invoked judgment (**Amos 3:15**). The eating of meat (lambs) with any regularity was the privilege of the wealthy. "The general population lived on wheat and barley and whatever fruits and vegetables were at hand, and if they had meat at all, reserved it for times of high celebration. … In contrast, Samaria's elite not only ate animals at random but also put their calves in special stalls to fatten them, undoubtedly on grain wrested from the poor" (Hubbard 193). Of course, Amos had earlier said that this luxury is obtained through robbery and violence against the poor (**3:10**).

The reclining (or lying down) and sprawling in **verses 4 and 7** depict not just comfort but drunken torpor—possibly of the religious kind like those mentioned in **Isaiah 65:11** and **Jeremiah 44:17**. The traditional custom in Israel at the time was to eat while sitting on rugs or seats. The practice of reclining at meals that Amos describes here is foreign. The Hebrew *sarach* (**sah-RAHKH**), translated "sprawl" (NLT), means to "go free, unrestrained," and is used in Arabic for camels left loose to pasture where they choose and of hair hanging loose (Snaith 112). Hubbard adds that it may also mean "free fall" from weakness or fatigue (Hubbarb 193). The word *parat* (Heb., **pah-RAHT**), generally translated "to chant," "to improvise," or "to sing extemporaneously," suggests a flow of trivial words in which the rhythm of words and music was everything but the sense and meaning nothing (Hubbard 193). Overall, scholars have concluded that this might have been a cultic banquet that was associated with specific deities and met periodically to celebrate with food and drink, and sometimes with sacred sexual orgies (Hubbard 192). These feasts were practiced for centuries across the Mediterranean basin and were known for their lavish consumption (Dunn 694). *Mizraq* (Heb., **miz-RAHK**) suggests that they used special bowls or basins for their wine-drinking, not ordinary cups. However we understand Amos' imagery, their parties featured extreme extravagance and careless ease.

The whole chapter pictures an upper class too self-centered and intent on its own pleasure as to find Amos' prediction of catastrophe credible. We see their apathy expressed in the clause, "they are not grieved for the affliction of Joseph," i.e., their own Northern Kingdom. Hubbard interprets this to say they have been sick for the wrong reasons: their drunkenness and their mourning of the dead (**6:9–10**). As they enjoyed all their luxuries, they had not even the slightest concern for the broken down state of the nation of Israel. Much like today, selfishness and greed caused people to only look for their own comfort, often at the expense of the needy.

7 Therefore now shall they go captive with the first that go captive, and the banquet of them that stretched themselves shall be removed. 8 The Lord GOD hath sworn by himself, saith the LORD the God of hosts, I abhor the excellency of Jacob, and hate his palaces: therefore will I deliver up the city with all that is therein.

The prophet's "therefore" begins to conclude the rebuke. Everything—all their drunken gluttonous orgies—will come to an end. Just as He rejects the sound of their worship (**Amos 5:21–24**), God also finds the noise of their amusement nauseous. These careless leaders of today will tomorrow lead the pitiful column of captives who go into exile. Thus, with tragic irony, Amos declares that they will be first to the bitter end. These notables of the "first of nations" (**v. 1**) who used "first quality oils" (**v. 6**) are now to be "first of the exiles." Where revelry filled the air, there shall remain only ominous silence (Mays 117). This prophecy emphasizes the unusually strong announcement of judgment that Amos also gives in **4:2** and **8:7**, "The Lord has sworn by himself." Mays observes, "That Yahweh takes oath on his own person (as in **Jeremiah 22:5, 49:13, 51:14**) makes the decree more final, because the total force of Yahweh's integrity is invested in this solemn oath—the ancient Near East's most binding form of commitment" (Mays 118).

The language used here is "the strongest possible language God used to express wrath … the language of abhorrence, hatred and chiasm" (Hubbard 195). The Lord abhors the "pride of Jacob." This pride of Jacob—which might actually be the city of Samaria (Dunn 694)—speaks of Israel's national self-confidence, which meant their displacement of Yahweh as the foundation of their national existence. However, God was about to judge their pride by sending an army that would bring them low. In addition, God hates the strongholds of Jacob—the strongholds that gave Israel a sense of self-sufficiency and security but were filled with the spoils of robbery and violence. They were like a monument before God as constant reminders of the pride of the rich and the plight of the poor. Mays adds, "The city and its strongholds…enshrines the worst of Israel's guilt. The powerful rich may think themselves invulnerable against any foe, but when Yahweh is against them, their strength is useless and their defenses already breached (Mays 119). This chapter concludes with the promise that God will raise up a nation against Israel to afflict them (**v. 14**). Assyria defeated Israel in 721/722 B.C., during the reign of King Hoshea of Israel.

QUESTIONS 1 & 2

What are the the signs of Israel's selfishness (**Amos 6:4–6**)?

What does the Lord despise and hate about Israel (v. 8)?

II. PUNISHMENT FOR THE SELF-INDULGENT (vv. 11–14)

The Lord has promised to enact severe punishment on Israel because of their refusal to repent. God will not only punish individuals, but plans to completely destroy their houses and buildings.

Disobedience and Destruction (verses 11–14)

11 For, behold, the LORD commandeth, and he will smite the great house with breaches, and the little house with clefts.

In judgment, God will smite the great house with breaches and the small house with clefts. Some scholars have said that the great house stands for Israel and the small house is Judah. For instance, Jerome interprets the former being reduced to branches or ruins, literally, "small drops"; the latter, though injured with "clefts" or rents, which threaten its fall, is still permitted to stand (Mays 120). Other scholars believe that "great house" and "small house" have nothing to do with Israel and Judah. This is because Amos primarily prophesied to the former and not the latter, and there is no other evidence of these terms being used for Israel and Judah. A better interpretation of the verse is that the judgment would come to both wealthy and poor. Why? Because rich and poor alike were guilty of turning away from Jehovah to serve their appetites. Destruction and death did not spare anyone.

12 Shall horses run upon the rock? will one plow there with oxen? for ye have turned judgment into gall, and the fruit of righteousness into hemlock: 13 Ye which rejoice in a thing of nought, which say, Have we not taken to us horns by our own strength?

Horses do not run on cliffs like mountain goats, nor can one plough through boulders with an ox. These are both absurd scenarios. In turning "justice into poison, and . . . righteousness into wormwood" (or hemlock, which is bitter and noxious), the Israelites were acting perversely. Thus, as horses and oxen are useless on a rock, so the Israelites are making justice poisonous. The absurd is happening in Israel. Arnold Schultz interprets this verse as saying, "There is a spiritual and moral order in the universe that is just as impossible to ignore as the natural order. It is as senseless to pervert justice as it is to expect horses to run on the rocks, or for oxen to plow on rock" (835). It is, thus, easier to change the course of nature than the course of God's providence or the laws of His just retribution.

The national leaders felt proud and confident because under Jeroboam, Israel had recaptured some territory that it had formerly lost to Aram (**2 Kings 14:25**). These recaptured lands included the town of Lodebar in Transjordan (**2 Samuel 9:4, 17:27**). Amos, however, cleverly made light of this feat by deliberately misspelling the city's name as "Lo-debar," which means "not a thing" (Mays 122). They had taken nothing of much value. The people were also claiming that they had taken the town of Karnaim (whose name means "a pair of horns," symbols of strength) by their own strength. It was not they but Yahweh, however, who had strengthened them to achieve this victory over a symbolically strong town. Therefore, Israel's leaders celebrate the capture of nothing and think they have captured it by their own strength (Mays 122).

14 But, behold, I will raise up against you a nation, O house of Israel, saith the LORD the God of hosts; and they shall afflict you from the entering in of Hemath unto the river of the wilderness.

Archaeological reports suggest that the capture was exactly and terribly fulfilled just as God had promised. Less than forty years after Amos wrote this prophecy, the Northern Kingdom was destroyed by Sargon of Assyria. "Behold" indicates God's resolute emphasis, as Yahweh had sworn by Himself (**v. 8**). God, through His power and sovereignty, raises up Sargon and the Assyrian empire to defeat and oppress the nation of Israel. "With power, he identifies himself as the Lord of all armies and with specificity, he directs his announcement to the whole house of Israel" (Hubbard 200). Selfishness, greed, and pride do not only affect the leaders of the nation; they affect everyone. The influence of Israel's leaders has corrupted the nation. Thus, the whole house of Israel is doomed to disaster by the complacency and corruption of their leaders.

BIBLE APPLICATION
AIM: Students will acknowledge that people of faith, responding to God's desire for justice, examine their ways of life.

In many places around the world, people are living in underserved and impoverished areas. They are suffering from lack of clean water, fresh produce, safe living conditions, and other resources that affect their everyday lives. There is not an equal distribution of wealth in our world. The powerful will continue to get rich, while the poor and working class will continue to suffer. The issue with wealth that is mentioned in this text is not the possession of wealth, but the dangers of being selfish, prideful, and sinful in the ways we use it. If we choose to ignore the injustices of the poor and needy, then we are at risk of God's punishment.

STUDENTS' RESPONSES
AIM: Students will discover that people of faith grieve and repent when God's people live unjustly.

We are tempted to ignore injustice because we are wealthy and comfortable. To combat this tendency, we can show solidarity with those who are disadvantaged. As a class, make a commitment to eat only one meal a day as an act of solidarity with those who live in hunger. While you are doing that, research ways in which you as a class can help fight global hunger. You can find many resources for this at the Bread for the World website (http://www.bread.org/help).

PRAYER
Lord, we do not always choose to love good, seek justice, and walk humbly before You. Thank You for another chance to love good, seek justice, and walk humbly before You. In the Name of Jesus. Amen.

DIGGING DEEPER
Rebuked for Selfishness
Lord GOD – What Does it Say in Hebrew? Did you notice the spelling of Lord God in verse 8? Why is God spelled in all capital letters? The explanation is found in the Hebrew behind our English translation.

The Hebrew word for God is Elohim. This Hebrew word for God is found over 2,500 times in Scripture. It is sometimes found in its abbreviated form, El. Hence, the name

Daniel means God is my judge, and Michael means Who is like God? Bethel means house of God. It is also found in compound forms. For example, El Elyon means God Most High (Gen 14:18-22), and El Shaddai is translated as God Almighty.

The Hebrew word translated Lord in our Bibles is Adonai. It means master, owner, and ruler. Accordingly, it refers to God as the one to whom all creation is subject. It is used some 300 times of God and 215 times of humans. When used in human relations, the word Adonai stresses dependence, submission, and even ownership.

When spelled in all capital letters, the word Lord is translated as the Hebrew name for God, YHWH (Exodus 3:14). It occurs 6,823 times in the Old Testament; it is the most frequent term used for God and is used only to refer to God. Most Bible scholars believe that it was originally pronounced Yahweh, although devout Jews will never attempt to pronounce the name out of reference to the divine name of God. Therefore, when reading the text, they will instead say Adonai and write Lord in all capital letters. When we see Lord in all capital letters, the Hebrew name behind it is YHWH.

Finally, with this information in mind, now we can explain the spelling in verse 8. The Hebrew behind the translation Lord GOD is YHWH Elohim.

HOW TO SAY IT

Lo-Debar.   lo-de-**BAR**.

Karnaim.   kar-**NAH**-yim.

YHWH   Yod-Heh-Waw-Heh

DAILY HOME BIBLE READINGS

MONDAY
Israel's Guilt and Punishment
(Amos 3:1–11)

TUESDAY
Jeroboam II's Reign
(2 Kings 14:23–28)

WEDNESDAY
Israel Carried Captive to Assyria
(2 Kings 17:5–23)

THURSDAY
Judah Carried Captive to Babylon
(2 Kings 25:1–21)

FRIDAY
Warning to Rich Oppressors
(James 5:1–6)

SATURDAY
The Deserted City
(Lamentations 1)

SUNDAY
God Has Got a Plan for This
(Jeremiah 29:10–14)

PREPARE FOR NEXT SUNDAY

Read **Amos 8:1–6, 9–10** and study "God Will Never Forget."

Sources:
Anderson, Francis I., and David Noel Freedman. *The Anchor Bible*. 1st Edition. New York: Doubleday, 1989.
Bitrus, Daniel. *Africa Bible Commentary*. Ed. Tokunboh Adeyemo. Grand Rapids, MI: Zondervan, 2006.
Boling, Robert G. *The Anchor Bible: Judges*. Vol. 6A. Garden City, NY: Doubleday & Company, Inc., 1975.
Dunn, James D. G., and J. W. Rogerson. *Eerdmans Commentary on the Bible*. Grand Rapids, MI: W.B. Eerdmans, 2003.
Gowan, Donald E. *The New Interpreter's Bible: A Commentary in Twelve Volumes*. Nashville, TN: Abingdon Press, 1996.
Hubbard, David Allan. *Joel and Amos: An Introduction and Commentary*. Downers Grove, IL: InterVarsity Press, 1989.
Mays, James Luther. *Amos: A Commentary*. Philadelphia: Westminster, 1969. Schultz, Arnold. *Wycliffe Bible Commentary*. Chicago: Moody Press, 1962. Snaith, Norman Henry. *The Book of Amos*. London: Epworth Press, 1945.

LESSON 5 • JUNE 29, 2025

GOD WILL NEVER FORGET

BIBLE BASIS: AMOS 8:1-6, 9-10

BIBLE TRUTH: Amos says that God will no longer overlook their misdeeds and will destroy them for all time.

MEMORY VERSE: "And he said, Amos, what seest thou? And I said, A basket of summer fruit. Then said the Lord unto me, The end is come upon my people of Israel; I will not again pass by them any more" (Amos 8:2).

LESSON AIM: By the end of the lesson, your students will: EXPLORE unjust practices and their consequences during Amos' time; REFLECT on how the church practices injustices and seems to be oblivious; ENCOURAGE the church to address injustices practiced within our community of faith.

BACKGROUND SCRIPTURE: Amos 8; Hosea 11:1-7—Read and incorporate the insights gained from the Background Scriptures into your study of the lesson.

LESSON SCRIPTURE

AMOS 8:1-6, 9-10, KJV

1 Thus hath the Lord GOD shewed unto me: and behold a basket of summer fruit.

2 And he said, Amos, what seest thou? And I said, A basket of summer fruit. Then said the LORD unto me, The end is come upon my people of Israel; I will not again pass by them any more.

3 And the songs of the temple shall be howlings in that day, saith the Lord GOD: there shall be many dead bodies in every place; they shall cast them forth with silence.

4 Hear this, O ye that swallow up the needy, even to make the poor of the land to fail,

5 Saying, When will the new moon be gone, that we may sell corn? And the sabbath, that we may set forth wheat, making the ephah small, and the shekel great, and falsifying the balances by deceit?

6 That we may buy the poor for silver, and the needy for a pair of shoes; yea, and sell the refuse of the wheat?

9 And it shall come to pass in that day, saith the Lord GOD, that I will cause the sun to go down at noon, and I will darken the earth in the clear day:

10 And I will turn your feasts into mourning, and all your songs into lamentation; and I will bring up sackcloth upon all loins, and baldness upon every head; and I will make it as the mourning of an only son, and the end thereof as a bitter day.

BIBLICAL DEFINITIONS

Lesson 4. A. Lamentation (Amos 8:10) *kinah* (Heb.)—Dirge, elegy.

B. Sackcloth (v. 10) *sak* (Heb.)—Rough woven cloth worn in humiliation and mourning.

LIFE NEED FOR TODAY'S LESSON

AIM: Students will learn to be careful and not allow their deceit and cheating of others to become their way of life and miss the

LESSON 5 • JUNE 29, 2025

warning signs of the consequences of their wicked ways.

INTRODUCTION
The Lord's Visions for Amos

The Lord gave Amos a series of visions that described Israel's complete destruction. The first vision that Amos receives is a swarm of locusts. These locusts would come at the most inopportune time, right after the king's portion had been harvested and the next crop was beginning to grow. If locusts came, then there would be a famine for the people. After Amos pleaded to spare the people, the Lord relented and showed him a devouring fire that consumed the land. Amos pleaded again and the Lord relented. Next Amos was shown a plumb line. This was a weight that builders used to make sure that walls were constructed properly. Israel would be shown to not be in line with God's standards and torn down. Before Amos could plead for God's mercy, the Lord confirmed that the nation of Israel would be judged.

Then Amos is confronted by Amaziah, the priest of Bethel. This confrontation results in Amos being charged with conspiracy against the king. Amos had denounced the legitimacy of the shrine at Bethel and the people's worship. As a result, Amaziah told Amos to go back to Judah and earn a living as a prophet there. Amos responds to this by stating that he is a farmer and a shepherd and that his prophetic calling is not for monetary gain, but a divine mandate from the Lord. He prophesies that Amaziah's family would die and that foreigners would claim his property. Amos adds that Amaziah himself would die in a foreign land. After this the Lord shows Amos a vision of a basket of ripe fruit and predicts the end of Israel.

BIBLE LEARNING
AIM: Students will know celebrations by the oppressors becomes clearly hypocritical and focused on selfish gain.

I. HUMAN GRIEF (Amos 8:1-3)

Amos' vision begins with a basket of summer fruit. This fruit was a symbol for Israel's impending judgment. The summer fruit was the fruit gathered in the harvest season. God was communicating a message to Israel through Amos: the time is ripe. The end had come for Israel and they were ripe for God's wrath. The Lord would spare them no longer. He could no longer offer them grace and show patience in the face of their persistent injustice and disobedience.

An Imminent Devastation (verses 1-3)

1 Thus hath the Lord GOD shewed unto me: and behold a basket of summer fruit. 2 And he said, Amos, what seest thou? And I said, A basket of summer fruit. Then said the LORD unto me, The end is come upon my people of Israel; I will not again pass by them any more. 3 And the songs of the temple shall be howlings in that day, saith the Lord GOD: there shall be many dead bodies in every place; they shall cast them forth with silence.

In the closing verses of **chapter** 7, Amos had confronted the priest Amaziah and pronounced an oracle of judgment against him for his failure to believe the Word of God (**Amos 7:16-17**). Now he resumes where he left off and continues the account of his visions. He begins by authenticating his fourth vision the same way as the previous ones, by declaring that the Lord showed him a vision (**7:1, 4, 7**). In the last vision in **7:7-9**, Amos declared that the end was certain but here he declares its imminence. The pres-

LESSON 5 • JUNE 29, 2025

ent vision is to reiterate and make final the previous one. He saw a basket of summer fruit (Heb. *qayits*, **KAH-yits**) and heard a response from the Lord that the "end" (Heb. *qets*, **KATES**) has come. Usually, summer fruit was not preserved but eaten as soon as it was gathered. So the Lord hints by this symbol and the pun on the word "end" that the kingdom of Israel was now ripe for destruction, and punishment must descend on it without delay. The Lord "will not again pass by them any more," that is, he will spare them no longer. However, the Hebrew word "end" here does not merely refer to its ripeness for judgment in a temporal sense, but its destruction and devastation.

There will be two responses. First, all the joy shall be turned into mourning. The songs of joy would be turned into yells, that is, into sounds of lamentation because of the multitude of the dead on the ground on every side. The word "howling" describes an inarticulate, shattering scream common during funerals, particularly in times of sudden devastation. Second, there will be silence, an appropriate response to God's severe judgment, accompanied by a destruction of untold proportions—"there shall be many dead bodies in every place."

QUESTION 1
What did God show Amos (**Amos 8:1**)?

II. COSMIC GRIEF (vv. 4–6, 9–10)

After the Lord shows them the grief they will experience, He shows them the reason for the coming judgment. They will be grieved because He has been grieved. He has put up with their trampling of the poor and needy. They anticipated the end of the New Moons and Sabbaths so they could go on cheating the people by selling inferior products and creating dishonest scales so they could make a profit. Instead of seeking justice for the poor, they sought ways to enslave them for negligible amounts of money: the price of sandals. They clearly had a low perspective on human life.

The Greedy Swallow Up the Needy (verses 4–6, 9–10)

4 Hear this, O ye that swallow up the needy, even to make the poor of the land to fail, 5 Saying, When will the new moon be gone, that we may sell corn? and the sabbath, that we may set forth wheat, making the ephah small, and the shekel great, and falsifying the balances by deceit? 6 That we may buy the poor for silver, and the needy for a pair of shoes; yea, and sell the refuse of the wheat?

Amos gives the reasons for the judgment and punishment. Israel failed to take care of its needy and poor, but instead exploited them and swallowed them up. The poor, vulnerable, and unprotected members of the society were treated harshly and unjustly. The rich grew richer on the back of the poor, and the poor became poorer. Yet these oppressive merchants kept going on with their religious activities, observing the Sabbath and other festivals. Worship, fraud, exploitation, and oppression went on simultaneously. Their worship was superficial, formal, and hypocritical. They detested the rest of the Sabbath, wanting to keep it as short as possible if they could, so as not to rest from their frauds. They considered the time spent for the festivals as business time lost. Amos quoted the merchants to show their attitude toward worship, "When will the new moon be gone, that we may sell corn and the Sabbath, that we may set forth wheat . . . ?" Their greed caused them to use deception to increase their profits. On the one hand, they reduced the weight, "made the ephah small," and on the other hand, they "made the shekel great," that is, increased the prices both ways by paring down the quantity which they sold and by obtaining more silver by fictitious weights, and weighing in uneven balances. Customers had no choice but to pay more than what the items they purchased were worth. Merchants bought the poor and confiscated their property as payment for debts. It sounds like modern-day "payday lending." Israel's sins are descriptive of our contemporary society.

For those living in the Western world, materialism is another god. Possessiveness is a great challenge. It is a world of opulence, one drowned in affluence. It raises several questions: At whose expense are we being enriched? Are workers being underpaid? What of those who rig the market, speculate with currency, or specialize in the financial subterfuge that falls only just short of outright theft? We must also remember that human greed for profit at the expense of the innocent destroys a society in the just desserts of divine repayment. It is indeed akin to a kind of religion, evoking profound love of self and happy acceptance of the ruin of others, neglecting God's command to love God and neighbors first (**Matthew 22:36–40**). But insatiable greed is so fundamentally foreign to the whole truth of God that it must not be tolerated but seriously condemned. But as Amos sees it, the foundations of avarice are so firm that only something earth-shattering could weaken its proud structures.

9 And it shall come to pass in that day, saith the Lord GOD, that I will cause the sun to go down at noon, and I will darken the earth in the clear day:

The first phrase "and it shall come to pass" in v. 9 translates the Hebrew word wehaya (**wehaw-YAH**), usually denoting that what follows as occurring in the future. "In that day" points to a time of the Lord's visitation to bring additional judgment and disasters on Israel. Israel needed to know that what was going to happen to them was the Day of the Lord. Amos refers to a devastation, namely a total eclipse of the sun. The Lord would create a day of darkness that would turn their merriment into misery, and transform their happy days into lamentation and mourning. The day of light would become a day of darkness, the eclipsed sun symbolizing that the light of God's face would be hidden from Israel. There are similar images of the Lord bringing darkness in times of judgment in several passages (see **Isaiah 59:10; Jeremiah 13:16, 15:9**). The imagery here of darkness on a clear day is shocking and symbolically expresses the sudden and unexpected end of Israel's prosperity and the darkening of her glory days, just when the nation seemed at its pinnacle of power. Nations today must be warned because God has not changed.

10 And I will turn your feasts into mourning, and all your songs into lamentation; and I will bring up sackcloth upon all loins, and baldness upon every head; and I will make it as the mourning of an only son, and the end thereof as a bitter day.

The consequences of Israel's failure to follow the Lord continue to reverberate in verse 10. Because of God's judgments, happy days will become harrowing days, festivals will be turned into mourning and joy to sadness. Because Israel had turned God's justice and righteousness into bitterness and poison (cf. 5:7; 6:12), He would turn their joy into grief. One cannot celebrate light and live in darkness. Baldness on every head suggests that every person in Israel would be touched by the grief-causing calamity. The Lord vowed to make the coming grief "like mourning for an only son." The loss of an only son produces an unspeakable grief. Such great sorrow attends the loss of an only son because not only is all

LESSON 5 • JUNE 29, 2025

hope for continuing one's family gone, but also the provision for one's old age (cf. **Jeremiah 6:26; Zechariah 12:10**). Mourning an only son is always a bitter experience—it is a picture of hopelessness. The day that starts out with mourning an only son is sure to end as bitter as it began. If we really desire the light of God to shine on us, then we must walk in the light.

QUESTIONS 2 and 3
When will God cause the sun to go down and what will happen to the earth (**v. 9**)?

What was God going to turn their feasts into (**v. 10**)?

BIBLE APPLICATION
AIM: Students will accept to live and obey God rather than to test God.

The profit motive drives most of what we do in a capitalist economy. While this has created many blessings for those with no opportunity, it has also created a culture in which we worship at the god of "profit." Whatever will sell, we will sell it regardless of whether it affects our fellow citizens negatively. As long as we can find a way to boost our finances, we buy and sell with no regard for the consequences. The Lord calls us to seek justice even in our commerce. These things brought judgment on the nation of Israel and may bring judgment on us as well.

STUDENTS' RESPONSES
AIM: Students will reflect on and analyze the root causes of injustice and their involvement in that injustice.

The greed and injustice of many corporate and business leaders is all around us if we open our eyes to see it. In the coming week, find an example online or in a newspaper of the ways that people's greed has led to oppression of the weak and vulnerable. Come back to class ready to share what you have discovered and an idea for combating this injustice.

PRAYER
Oh God! You brought us through so many troubled waters of racism, economic exploitation, and other isms. Yet, we do not always honor and worship You for all of the many blessings You have given us, and the justice that has prevailed in our lives. Help us and keep focused on Your justice and not just-us. In Jesus' Name we pray. Amen.

DIGGING DEEPER:

What Did You See? How Old Testament Prophets Received Their Messages

How did the prophets receive the messages they would proclaim to his hearers? One manner is through sight. In Amos 8:1, the prophet says the Lord God showed him the prophecy. Other prophets have similar experiences.

> The **vision** of Isaiah, the son of Amoz, which he **saw** ... (Isaiah 1:1).

> The word that Isaiah, the son of Amoz, **saw** concerning Judah and Jerusalem (Isaiah 2:1).

> The word of the Lord that came to Micah ... which he **saw** concerning Samaria and Jerusalem (Micah 1:1).

> In the thirtieth year, in the fourth month, on the fifth day of the month, as I was among the exiles by the Chebar canal, the heavens were opened, and **I saw visions** of God (Ezekiel 1:1).

On the other hand, the false prophets have not seen visions from God. As a matter of fact, Ezekiel is explicit in stating:

> They have seen false visions and lying divination. They say, "Declares the Lord," when the Lord has not sent them, and yet they expect him to fulfill their word (Ezekiel 13:6; cf. Jeremiah 14:13-14).

LESSON 5 • JUNE 29, 2025

The Lord can also communicate directly with the prophet. No medium is indicated – only that the word of the Lord came to the prophet. For example, after delivering the news of impending death upon Hezekiah, the Bible says:

> Before Isaiah had gone out of the middle court, the word of the LORD came to him (2 Kings 20:4).

HOW TO SAY IT

Amaziah.   am-uh-ZEE-uh.

Ephah.   ee-FAH.

DAILY HOME BIBLE READINGS

MONDAY
A Famine of Hearing God's Word
(Amos 8:11–14)

TUESDAY
Reaping the Whirlwind
(Hosea 8:7–14)

WEDNESDAY
Days of Punishment Have Come
(Hosea 9:5–9)

THURSDAY
Israel's Sin Shall Be Destroyed
(Hosea 10:1–8)

FRIDAY
Israel Refused to Return to Me
(Hosea 11:1–7)

SATURDAY
God Will Remember Their Iniquity
(Jeremiah 14:1–10)

SUNDAY
A Day of Mourning and Lamentation
(Amos 8:1–6, 9–10)

PREPARE FOR NEXT SUNDAY

Read **Micah 2:4–11** and study "No Rest for the Wicked."

Sources:
Achtemmeier, Elizabeth. *Minor Prophets 1.* Understanding the Bible Commentary Series. Grand Rapids, MI: Baker Books, 1996.
Craigie, Peter C. *Twelve Prophets.* The Daily Study Bible Series. Vol. 1. Louisville, KY: Westminster John Knox Press, 1984.
Nogalski, James D. *The Book of the Twelve: Hosea–Jonah.* Macon, GA: Smyth and Helwys Publishing, Inc., 2011.
Smith, Billy K., and Franklin S. Page. *Amos, Obadiah, Jonah.* The New American Commentary. Vol. 19B. Nashville, TN: Broadman & Holman Publishers, 1995.
Stuart, Douglas. *Hosea–Jonah.* Word Biblical Commentary. Vol. 31. Dallas: Word Publishers, 2002.
de Waard, Jan, and William Allen Smalley. *A Translator's Handbook on the Book of Amos.* UBS Handbook Series. Stuttgart, Germany: United Bible Societies, 1979.

COMMENTS / NOTES:

LESSON 6 • JULY 6, 2025

NO REST FOR THE WICKED

BIBLE BASIS: MICAH 2:4–11

BIBLE TRUTH: God gives no rest to those who practice evil against His faithful ones.

MEMORY VERSE: "O thou that art named the house of Jacob, is the spirit of the LORD straitened? are these his doings? do not my words do good to him that walketh uprightly?" (Micah 2:7).

LESSON AIM: By the end of the lesson, your students will: EXPLORE Micah's depiction of people who deny their wrongdoing in the community; EXPRESS feelings about people who attempt to justify the evil and harm they commit; and RESPOND with appropriate opposition to those engaged in wrongdoing in the community.

BACKGROUND SCRIPTURE: Micah 2; Proverbs 11:1-10—Read and incorporate the insights gained from the Background Scriptures into your study of the lesson.

LESSON SCRIPTURE

MICAH 2:4–11, KJV

4 In that day shall one take up a parable against you, and lament with a doleful lamentation, and say, We be utterly spoiled: he hath changed the portion of my people: how hath he removed it from me! turning away he hath divided our fields.

5 Therefore thou shalt have none that shall cast a cord by lot in the congregation of the LORD.

6 Prophesy ye not, say they to them that prophesy: they shall not prophesy to them, that they shall not take shame.

7 O thou that art named the house of Jacob, is the spirit of the LORD straitened? are these his doings? do not my words do good to him that walketh uprightly?

8 Even of late my people is risen up as an enemy: ye pull off the robe with the garment from them that pass by securely as men averse from war.

9 The women of my people have ye cast out from their pleasant houses; from their children have ye taken away my glory for ever.

10 Arise ye, and depart; for this is not your rest: because it is polluted, it shall destroy you, even with a sore destruction.

11 If a man walking in the spirit and falsehood do lie, saying, I will prophesy unto thee of wine and of strong drink; he shall even be the prophet of this people.

BIBLICAL DEFINITIONS

A. Parable (Micah 2:4) *mashal* (Heb.)—A **proverb or byword.**

B. Prophesy (v. 11) *nataf* (Heb.)—To cause to drip or make words flow.

LIFE NEED FOR TODAY'S LESSON

AIM: Students will learn that people do not want to be confronted with their social and moral abuse of others.

INTRODUCTION

God Rewards the Oppressors

Micah ministered during a time in which Assyria enjoyed great power and influence. The Northern Kingdom of Israel had already fallen. King Ahaz of Judah made an arrangement with Assyria to prevent the fall of Judah. The Southern Kingdom would pay large tribute and honor Assyria's gods. As a result, idol worship spread throughout Judah.

Samaria would be destroyed. The walls would be broken down, the foundations would be laid bare, and vineyards would be planted where their streets once were (**Micah 1:6**). Her destruction came in 722 B.C., after a three year siege by the Assyrian army.

The Lord also names specific cities in Judah where His judgment will be visited. The Lord gives His reasons for His judgment against Judah: the greed and covetousness of the rich and the oppression of the lower class.

Micah 2 begins with the description of the deeds of the wealthy land barons and their wanton greed. The rich seized the houses and land of the poor and stole their possessions. The Lord promises to reward their evil with evil and that the oppressors would themselves be oppressed.

BIBLE LEARNING
AIM: Students will discover that Micah confronted those whose evil actions resulted in the suffering of innocent people.

1. THE LAND DIVIDED (Micah 2:4–5)
The rich were getting richer at the expense of the poor. Greedy land barons were confiscating the lands, homes, and goods of the poor. The Lord promised judgment for this injustice, and tells them that they will suffer the same injustice (**vv. 4–5**). Assyria would confiscate the lands, homes, and goods that the rich had taken. Further, they would taunt Judah with their own lamentations.

Justice is Served! (verses 4–5)
4 In that day shall one take up a parable against you, and lament with a doleful lamentation, and say, We be utterly spoiled: he hath changed the portion of my people: how hath he removed it from me! turning away he hath divided our fields. 5 Therefore thou shalt have none that shall cast a cord by lot in the congregation of the LORD.

Beginning with **verse 2**, the prophet Micah presents a portrait of God's reversal of Judah's situation. In **verses 1–2**, the oppressing classes ruined others; they had used violence to deprive others of their possessions and take the fields of the poor. Now in **verse 4**, the tables are turned: the oppressors will become the oppressed, and their enemies will divide up their land. The Lord will take the fields away from the scheming land-grabbers in Israel, and give them to the treacherous Assyrians. The rich had seized the fields of their helpless victims (**v. 2**); now the Lord will take those fields and turn them over to enemies. So the rich are dispossessed of their ill-gotten property. Micah quotes the rich as saying, "We be utterly spoiled: he hath changed the portion of my people: how hath he removed it from me!" When the disaster comes, the rich landowners will be mocked. "Men will ridicule you" (NIV) is literally "he will lift up against you a parable." The Hebrew word *mashal* (**maw-SHAWL**), translated as "parable," is used here with the negative sense of a byword.

The prophet speaks on behalf of God (**v. 5**). He uses the word "therefore" to link this verse with the preceding verses, showing both the result and extent of the judgment. In the Old Testament, there were two ways in which land was returned to its original owner: first in the year of Jubilee (**Leviticus 25**), second by lot at the time of Joshua (**Joshua 14:2**), a practice that continued and was alluded to in **Psalm 16:6** (KJV). The latter is what Micah refers to here. The families of the oppressors will have no representation. The punishment fits the crime. What a solemn warning against greed, materialism and oppression. Because the guilty parties have dealt with their neighbors' fields unjustly, none of their descendants will be left in the Lord's covenant community who can use a cord (measuring line) to divide up the land by lot. So they will be cut off from the promises of the Lord's people. They will have no one to claim their inheritance, either because their family will be completely wiped out or they will all be in exile. People who have a desperate greed for land and material wealth turn their personal goals into their god, but such people will also learn the emptiness of riches, lands, and materials at their loss.

QUESTION 1
How does the Lord punish Judah for their evil practices (**Micah 2:4–5**)?

II. THE LORD INCITED (vv. 6–9)
The people of Judah had no interest in Micah's message of judgment. "Don't prophesy like that," they said. They did not believe that any calamity would befall them. During this time, there were false prophets in Judah that only prophesied peace and blessing. The wealthy people of Judah preferred to hear the false messages. They did not want to hear any prophecies that exposed their faults or demanded change.

Micah—Stop Talking! (verses 6–9)

6 Prophesy ye not, say they to them that prophesy: they shall not prophesy to them, that they shall not take shame. 7 O thou that art named the house of Jacob, is the spirit of the LORD straitened? are these his doings? do not my words do good to him that walketh uprightly?

How true is the axiom that truth hurts! It is hardly surprising that Micah's stern message to the rich did not bring him popularity. The message sounded offensive to them, so they commanded him to stop saying such things as he had said in **2:1–5**. The verb used for prophesy is *nataf* (Heb., **naw-TAWF**), which means "to drip." Used in this context, it has a connotation of driveling or foaming at the mouth. The false prophets are really telling the Lord's prophets, "Stop foaming at the mouth," which shows their scorn for the message. The same is true today: charlatans reject all judgment, prophecy, and proclamation. They could not believe that disaster and disgrace would overtake them because they thought God would not do such things. It was, to them, a figment of Micah's imagination, but they were wrong. The greedy oppressors were confident that no evil would trouble them.

Micah's opponents used rhetorical questions to say, "Do not even mention judgment. God is not annoyed." The word *qatsar* (Heb., **kaw-TSAR**), translated "straitened" (KJV), literally means "short." Here Micah turns the words of the evildoers against them by asking of the Lord is "short of spirit," an idiom for "impatient" or "quick-tempered." The false prophets were teaching erroneously that the Lord's patience had no limits (cf. **Exodus 34:6–7a**). They cannot believe that the Lord would really lose His patience, especially with them. Surely, He must be able to put up easily with them despite their sins. So, they asked, "Is the Lord short-tempered," "Does the Lord get angry quickly?" Without waiting for an answer, they ask another question, "Are these things that you say will happen the deeds of God?" The final question admits that God is righteous, but if this question comes from the mouths of the oppressors, it shows that they assume that they also are among those who walk uprightly, and can thus expect that God will speak kindly to them. This assumption underlines their moral blindness. The point is that God's words or promises cause good to happen to the one who walks uprightly.

8 Even of late my people is risen up as an enemy: ye pull off the robe with the garment from them that pass by securely as men averse from war. 9 The women of my people have ye cast out from their pleasant houses; from their children have ye taken away my glory for ever.

Micah continues to describe the offenses of his hearers. He lists the specific sins of the people. God calls them "my people." However, their behavior did not reflect that of those that belong to God. It was a sad case of God's people living ungodly lives. He said, "Even of late," that is, only recently you have pulled off the robe of those who walked securely and men who were averse to war, a reference to the innocent and peaceful travellers. The women and children were not spared the humiliation and atrocities. The former were driven away from their houses, suggesting that these women might have been widows. The wealthy not only dispossessed women but also disinherited their children. Thus, the children were left without property, money, or security. Doubtless, a society could not be in a lower state of morality than when it oppresses and exploits the vulnerable in it. Micah's denouncements retain a pressing relevance in a world where such conditions continue. Covetousness and greed still have the same devastating results for defenseless women and children and the unprotected poor. For those who are called Christians, it is important that our character mirrors that of Christ.

QUESTION 2
What evil does the Lord judge them for (vv. 8–9)?

III. THE LIES INVITED (vv. 10–11)
The Lord gives His sentence against Judah: "Up! Begone! This is no longer your land and home, for you have filled it with sin and ruined it completely" (**v. 10**). The powerful land barons would be evicted from the very property they had stolen. In the same way that they stripped the poor, widows, and orphans of their lands and possessions, the Lord would strip them.

The Destiny of the Rich is Sealed (verses 10–11)

10 Arise ye, and depart; for this is not your rest: because it is polluted, it shall destroy you, even with a sore destruction.

This verse takes up again the theme of **verse 4** and announces the fate of the rich oppressors. The rich must get up and go into exile. The oppressors among God's people rose up like an enemy to increase their wealth and power at the expense of others among their own people; now the Lord tells them to prepare to leave their ill-gotten land and possessions behind. They who had evicted others from their land were about to be evicted themselves; they would go away into exile. Their wrongfully acquired land will no longer be their possession. The reason is that they defiled it with their sins and ruined it beyond all remedy. Others will take over their property acquired by fraud and oppression.

11 If a man walking in the spirit and falsehood do lie, saying, I will prophesy unto thee of wine and of strong drink; he shall even be the prophet of this people.

The section ends in **verse 11** as the prophet returns to practice of false prophecy. Micah says that his hearers are so deluded that if a preacher or prophet were to come along preaching the gospel of wine and strong drink, or prosperity gospel as we know it today, they would hire him immediately. Here, such a prophet is called a liar and deceiver, obviously because he does not tell the truth and so leads others astray. His message is one of peace and prosperity, "plenty of wine and beer" (NIV). The sinful, covenant-breaking

LESSON 6 • JULY 6, 2025

people deserve that kind of prophet. Anyone who promises greater affluence will gain a hearing. False prophets are happy to oblige with "feel-good messages" so long as their hearers feed them and fill the coffers of the church or ministry with money (**3:5, 11**). The tests of true prophets are given in **Deuteronomy 13:1–3, 18:17–22**: A prophet's message must not contradict or disagree with the previous revelation of truth through true prophets (cf. **Isaiah 8:19–20**), and his predictions must come true. These prophets failed on both counts.

Today there are still false prophets and teachers both inside and outside the church. In recent years, some preachers throughout the world have not only made predictions about the coming of the Lord but also about those who might be elected to certain political offices. Unfortunately they have been proven wrong. There are still swindlers and hucksters who "peddle the word of God for profit" (**2 Corinthians 2:17, NIV**). Jesus issued a warning about them (**Matthew 24:4–5, 10–11, 23–24**); so did Paul and John (**1 Timothy 4:1–2; 1 John 2:18–19, 4:1–3**). Such so-called ministers may masquerade as "apostles of Christ," but in reality they are "false apostles" and servants of Satan (**2 Corinthians 11:13–15**). They will exist as long as there are people who "will gather around them a great number of teachers to say what their itching ears want to hear" (from **2 Timothy 4:3**).

QUESTION 3
What is the message the people would like to hear (**v. 11**)?

BIBLE APPLICATION
AIM: Students will affirm that God is in control despite the presence of evil and suffering.

The effects of greed can be felt throughout our society. Corporations have crushed the lives of countless people in their quest to make a profit. As a society, we have sought luxuries at the expense of workers and their wages. We put our material comforts ahead of justice for others. God is not pleased with this. Instead of wanting to hear the truth, we would rather hear preachers tell us about how much more money we are going to get or what expensive house or car God is going to give us. The Lord wants us to repent of our evil ways so we can hear the truth and seek justice for the oppressed.

STUDENTS' RESPONSES
AIM: Students will step out in God's power to speak and act for justice.

Greed was the driving force behind Judah's unjust ways. So often, the world prompts us to get all we can, even at the expense of others. Instead God calls us to seek out the welfare of the poor and weak. One way that we can do that is fight against modern slavery. Take some time to learn more about the conditions and what you can do at the "Not For Sale" website (http://www.notforsalecampaign.org/about/ slavery/slavery-faq).

PRAYER
Jesus, we seek to learn more or grow deeper in what we do for others. Lord, let us be receptive to people caring for us when we are in need, so that we in turn will be refreshed and ready to care for others. In Jesus' Name we pray. Amen.

DIGGING DEEPER:
You Need to Stop

"Shut up, preacher!" That's what the people said to the prophet as he declared God's message of eventual judgment. Modern translations help the read to identify where the false prophets are being quoted and Micah's response.

False prophets (v. 6): *"Do not preach! One should not preach of such things; disgrace will not overtake us."* Isaiah had the same experience of being silenced. The Lord says of them:

> They are a rebellious people, lying children, children unwilling to hear the instruction of the Lord, who say to the seers, "Do not see," and to the prophets, "Do not prophesy to us what is right; speak to us smooth things, prophesy illusions, leave the way turn aside from the path, let us hear no more about the Holy One of Israel" **(Isaiah 30:10).**

Verses 5-13 record Micah's continued woe against the wicked.

Clearly, these are false prophets. The Lord warned his people in advance that they would come among the people. In love, he gave them criteria to identify them.

> *If you say in your heart, "How may we know the word that the Lord has not spoken?"* **[Answer:]** *When a prophet speaks in the name of the Lord, if the word does not come to pass or come true, that is a word that the Lord has not spoken; the prophet has spoken it presumptuously. You need not be afraid of him* **(Deuteronomy 18:21-22).**

HOW TO SAY IT

Doleful.	**DOL**-ful.
Averse.	a-**VERS**.

DAILY HOME BIBLE READINGS

MONDAY
Good Deeds for the Oppressed
(Job 29:7–17)

TUESDAY
Attention to the Needs of Others
(Job 31:13–22)

WEDNESDAY
Judge Me, O Lord
(Psalm 7:1–8)

THURSDAY
Test My Mind and Heart
(Psalm 7:9–17)

FRIDAY
The Lord Executes Judgment
(Psalm 9:15–20)

SATURDAY
The Righteous and the Wicked
(Proverbs 11:1–10)

SUNDAY
A Day of Bitter Lamentation
(Micah 2:4–11)

PREPARE FOR NEXT SUNDAY

Read **Micah 3:5–12** and study "No Tolerance for Corrupt Leaders and Prophets."

Sources:

Allen, Leslie C. *The Books of Joel, Obadiah, Jonah and Micah*. New International Commentary of the Old Testament. Grand Rapids, MI: Wm. B. Eerdmans, 1976.

Barker, Kenneth L. *Micah, Nahum, Habakkuk, Zephaniah*. The New American Commentary. Vol. 20. Nashville, TN: Broadman & Holman Publishers, 1999.

Boice, J. M. *The Minor Prophets*. 2 vols. Complete in one edition. Grand Rapids, MI: Kregel, 1996.

Clark, David J. and Norm Mundhenk. *A Translator's Handbook on the Book of Micah*, UBS Handbook Series. London: United Bible Societies, 1982.

Craigie, P. C. *Twelve Prophets*. 2 vols. Philadelphia: Westminster, 1985. S.v. 2:19. Dockery, David S., ed. *Holman Concise Bible Commentary*. Nashville, TN: Broadman & Holman Publishers, 1998.

Easton, M. G. *Easton's Bible Dictionary*. New York: Harper & Brothers, 1893. Feinberg, Charles L. *The Minor Prophets*. Chicago: Moody Press, 1976.

Henry, Matthew. *Matthew Henry's Commentary on the Whole Bible: Complete and Unabridged in One Volume*. Peabody, MA: Hendrickson, 1994.

Jamieson, Robert, A. R. Fausset and David Brown. *Commentary Critical and Explanatory on the Whole Bible*. Oak Harbor, WA: Logos Research Systems, Inc., 1997.

Myers, Allen C. *The Eerdmans Bible Dictionary*. Grand Rapids, MI: Eerdmans, 1987.

Smith, James E. *The Minor Prophets*. Old Testament Survey Series. Joplin, MO: College Press, 1994.

Smith, Ralph L. *Micah–Malachi*. Word Biblical Commentary. Vol. 32. Dallas: Word, Incorporated, 1998.

Walvoord, John F., Roy B. Zuck, and Dallas Theological Seminary. *The Bible Knowledge Commentary: An Exposition of the Scriptures*. Wheaton, IL: Victor Books, 1985.

COMMENTS / NOTES:

LESSON 7 • JULY 13, 2025

NO TOLERANCE FOR CORRUPT LEADERS AND PROPHETS

BIBLE BASIS: MICAH 3:5-12

BIBLE TRUTH: God will judge and punish corrupt leaders and prophets.

MEMORY VERSE: "But truly I am full of power by the spirit of the LORD, and of judgment, and of might, to declare unto Jacob his transgression, and to Israel his sin" (Micah 3:8).

LESSON AIM: By the end of the lesson, your students will: EXPLORE how Micah confronted corrupt leaders; REFLECT on reactions to leaders who mislead and deceive people; and ADDRESS corruptions in leadership within the church and the broader community.

BACKGROUND SCRIPTURE: Micah 3; Matthew 7:15-20—Read and incorporate the insights gained from the Background Scriptures into your study of the lesson.

LESSON SCRIPTURE

MICAH 3:5-12, KJV

5 Thus saith the LORD concerning the prophets that make my people err, that bite with their teeth, and cry, Peace; and he that putteth not into their mouths, they even prepare war against him.

6 Therefore night shall be unto you, that ye shall not have a vision; and it shall be dark unto you, that ye shall not divine; and the sun shall go down over the prophets, and the day shall be dark over them.

7 Then shall the seers be ashamed, and the diviners confounded: yea, they shall all cover their lips; for there is no answer of God.

8 But truly I am full of power by the spirit of the LORD, and of judgment, and of might, to declare unto Jacob his transgression, and to Israel his sin.

9 Hear this, I pray you, ye heads of the house of Jacob, and princes of the house of Israel, that abhor judgment, and pervert all equity.

10 They build up Zion with blood, and Jerusalem with iniquity.

11 The heads thereof judge for reward, and the priests thereof teach for hire, and the prophets thereof divine for money: yet will they lean upon the LORD, and say, Is not the LORD among us? none evil can come upon us.

12 Therefore shall Zion for your sake be plowed as a field, and Jerusalem shall become heaps, and the mountain of the house as the high places of the forest.

BIBLICAL DEFINITIONS

A. Confounded (Micah 3:7) *khafer* (Heb.)—To be ashamed, to be embarrassed.

B. Equity (v. 9) *yashar* (Heb.)—Upright, straight, level.

LESSON 7 • JULY 13, 2025

LIFE NEED FOR TODAY'S LESSON
AIM: Students will affirm that some leaders are corrupt and lie to the people they are charged to protect.

INTRODUCTION
Deceptive Rulers
The Neo-Assyrian Empire was a very dominant and real threat to Jerusalem at Micah's time. One of many ways Jerusalem prepared for conflict was to strengthen the economy so they would have the necessary resources to fight off both foreign and domestic threats. As today's text suggests, the ways they pursued economic stability were immoral and did not align with the precepts of the Lord. Their stimulus plan was based on greed, exploitation, and senseless taxes, and as a result, moral corruption slowly crept in.

BIBLE LEARNING
AIM: Students will understand that sins against others affect their relationship with God.

I. Corrupt Prophets (Micah 3:5-7)
Micah is speaking on behalf of God and unveiling the sinister practices of the prophets in Jerusalem and Samaria. Micah not only classifies them as deceivers, but specifically identifies their transgressions (wrongdoings). War was imminent and the prophets were capitalizing on Jerusalem's concerns by structuring their messages to benefit their paying audience, while those who could not pay received detrimental messages.

Oppressive Prophets (verses 5-7)
5 Thus saith the LORD concerning the prophets that make my people err, that bite with their teeth, and cry, Peace; and he that putteth not into their mouths, they even prepare war against him.

After an analogy comparing the leaders of Judah to cannibalistic shepherds, Micah then focuses on Judah's prophets, who are causing the people to err (Heb. *ta'ah*, **ta-AH**) or wander. The prophets were causing the people to go astray and wander from God and His truth—the opposite of their true role as spokesmen for God. Instead of speaking for God, they are speaking on their own and drawing people away from God. Micah says that they "bite with their teeth." The word "bite" can also be used figuratively as "to vex" and "to oppress." The prophets were vexing and oppressing the people by offering prophecies for money. This is further confirmed by the next clause. The word "putteth" (Heb. *natan*, **na-TAN**) is more often rendered "to give." The prophets' message of peace was their selling point; they told the people that everything would be well and received the people's money and applause. However, this was a false peace; those who would not give to them would be the objects of their hostility.

6 Therefore night shall be unto you, that ye shall not have a vision; and it shall be dark unto you, that ye shall not divine; and the sun shall go down over the prophets, and the day shall be dark over them.

As a result of their false prophecies and oppression, God would judge the prophets, manifesting itself in their lack of prophetic sight. Micah says that the prophets will experience darkness, and they will not be able to divine (Heb. *qasam*, **kah-SAM**). Divination was a common way to understand the will of the gods. This was done through various methods; some would read and interpret the liver of animals or the position of fired arrows, while others studied dreams and visions. The latter is probably the method used by these false prophets of Judah. The sun going down and the day turning dark are metaphors for the loss of the prophet's gifts.

7 Then shall the seers be ashamed, and the diviners confounded: yea, they shall all cover their lips; for there is no answer of God.

Micah announces the fate of the seers (Heb. *chozeh*, **kho-ZEH**) and diviners (Heb. *qasam*, **kah-SAM**): they will be ashamed and confounded, and experience the humiliation of lepers by having to cover their lips (**Leviticus 13:45**). The prophets would be considered unclean like lepers because they had "no answer of God." Their lack of honesty and true relationship with God would be evident. Because their falsehood was on display, they would cover their lips and feel the same shame as those considered outcasts to the covenant community.

QUESTION 1
What were the prophets doing to the people (**Micah 3:5**)?

II. THE MAN OF GOD (vv. 8–10)

Amid all of this, Micah stands up for justice. He proclaims his strength and courage so all will know he knows the depth of their corruption. He also informs them he understands the magnitude of the danger that he is in by speaking out. The eighth century B.C. was not very different from today's society as far as the extent of corruption; someone seeking to change the economic and social structure would face social, political, and religious opposition much as Jesus, Medgar Evers, and Martin Luther King Jr. did.

A True Prophet of God (verses 8–10)

8 But truly I am full of power by the spirit of the LORD, and of judgment, and of might, to declare unto Jacob his transgression, and to Israel his sin.

Micah declares his distinction from the false prophets. He says that he is full of power (Heb. *koach*, **KOH-akh**) by the spirit of the Lord. He is also full of judgment (Heb. *mishpat*, **mishPAWT**) and might (Heb. *geburah*, **geh-vooRAH**). Micah's "judgment" here is the establishment of right through fair and legal procedures in accordance with the will and laws of God. Micah has aligned himself with the cause of justice, and by using the word's power and might, he states that this cause is God's cause and he is equipped to be victorious.

9 Hear this, I pray you, ye heads of the house of Jacob, and princes of the house of Israel, that abhor judgment, and pervert all equity.

Micah particularly addresses the political and religious groups of Judah. He calls out the heads and princes responsible for establishing the religious and political moral standards for the people. The Lord, through Micah, accuses them of hating or abhorring what is just. The word "abhor," or *ta'ab* (Heb., **tah-AV**, to loathe, detest, or make abominable) is a strong indication of how far those who rule over the Hebrews have fallen from God. They are not instructing people with fairness, but seeking their own gain and pursuing personal agendas.

Not only do these rulers and chiefs abhor justice, they also pervert equity (Heb. *yashar*, **yah-SHAWR**, that which is straight, right, or just). This word also denotes fairness and being honest and aboveboard. Those who rule over Judah do not practice such honesty.

10 They build up Zion with blood, and Jerusalem with iniquity.

The prophet continues to personalize the accusation against Judah. In the name of religion and sacrifice to God, the people have erected buildings using perverse and deceitful means. Instead of using tithes and offerings to establish places of worship, the religious leaders have taken from the poor and, in some instances, killed to expand Jerusalem. Archaeology testifies to the building activities underway in Jerusalem during Micah's prophecy. Such capital activities were performed at the expense of the oppressed and less fortunate. Jeremiah makes reference to similar activities, mentioning those who build their homes by unrighteousness (**22:13**). The prophet Habakkuk (**2:12**) also records official building with bloodshed.

The name "Zion" refers to the hill between the Kidron and Tyropean valleys that David captured from the Jebusites (**2 Samuel 5:7**). After the building of the temple to the north of the hill, Zion became the center of the Lord's activity, since the temple was where Yahweh dwelt. The term "Zion" may refer specifically to the temple vicinity or Jerusalem in general. Thus, Micah's reference to the people building Zion up with blood shows how this holy habitation had been defamed and desecrated.

III. CORRUPT LEADERS (vv. 11–12)

Micah says the leaders are attempting to build up the city, but at the expense of the poor. There was no respect for justice or righteousness. The false prophets were not the only corrupt citizens in Samaria and Jerusalem; leaders in almost every area of their society had gone astray (**vv. 9–12**). As a nation and individually for many leaders, the focus quickly became prosperity by any means necessary.

Corrupt Leaders of Judah (verses 11–12)

11 The heads thereof judge for reward, and the priests thereof teach for hire, and the prophets thereof divine for money: yet will they lean upon the LORD, and say, Is not the LORD among us? none evil can come upon us.

Micah again compels Judah to reexamine its political and social ethics. The rulers who govern civic and state affairs are corrupt. The priests who dictate religious standards practice evil. The prophets who speak the Word of the Lord only do it for money. Micah contends that Judah's leadership have turned away from the Lord. Those in power only want to be compensated by humankind for what God has gifted and instructed them to do. Rulers give judgment for a bribe, priests teach for a price, and prophets give oracles for money. Micah stresses the greed and insatiable materialism pervading Judah.

These leaders, however, believe that what they do is good and pleasing in the eyes of the Lord. They are convinced that since Zion is the dwelling place of God and that since the Hebrews are God's chosen people, all is well and their transgressions can be overlooked. Speaking rhetorically, Micah states that those in authority did not lean on the Lord. The word "lean" (Heb. *sha'an*, **shah-AWN**), means to lie, rely on, or rest on, often with reference to God (**2 Chronicles 14:11**). Isaish uses another verb for leaning in stating how Judah must depend on God (**48:2**). Such leaning implies a need to find favor and obtain support. Judah wishes to engage in wrongdoing while depending on the Lord for safety. The leaders, despite their unscrupulous conduct, believe that God will protect them because of His faithfulness and promises. The people do not see the error of their ways; they are so obstinate and spiritually blind that they are convinced that because the Lord dwells in Zion, no harm can come to them even when they sin against God.

12 Therefore shall Zion for your sake be plowed as a field, and Jerusalem shall become heaps, and the mountains of the house as the high places in the forest.

Because Judah has become prideful and sinful, the Lord, through Micah, predicts its ensuing destruction. The crassness of the leaders will result in the leveling of Jerusa-

LESSON 7 • JULY 13, 2025

lem and its temple. Micah made a similar pronouncement earlier stating that Samaria would be a heap and a place for planting vineyards, i.e., a desolate, open land (**1:6**). This prophecy is remembered a century later when the people of Israel observe its fulfillment (**Jeremiah 26:18-19**). Both prophets were foretelling the captivity of Judah by the Babylonians and the exile afterward. Judah, during Micah's time, was already a vassal state of the Assyrians; further enslavement was the next step.

Again the prophet specifically names Zion and Jerusalem, the center of Israelite worship, as places to be destroyed. No place was beyond God's wrath when evil had been committed. Micah personalizes the message and the plans of God to show Judah's leaders their ill behavior.

QUESTION 2
Based on Micah's prophecy, what was the primary source of motivation during this period in Jerusalem (**v. 11**)?

BIBLE APPLICATION
AIM: Students will realize that the truth must always be told, even if the message is not a pleasant one.

It can be very difficult to speak against leadership at any level. Some people naturally believe that if someone has been given a title or responsibility, they have integrity and will maintain the best interest of the people they represent. However, the Bible and life have provided us with many examples of leaders who have ill intentions, succumb to temptation, and take advantage of their positions. As children of God, our instructions are simple: do justice, love kindness, and walk humbly with our God (**Micah 6:8**). Every group that we are members of—our country, civic organization, religious institution, or sorority/fraternity—should follow the same statutes.

STUDENTS' RESPONSES
AIM: Students will find comfort in knowing that God will bring justice where there is corruption.

After reading the Lesson in Our Society, discuss what we should do as Christians if we suspect a political leader is corrupt. Make a list of appropriate and inappropriate response methods. One way to respond is to confront the leader and withhold votes or cooperation with unjust policies and practices. With this in mind, consider your own community and whether this response is needed.

PRAYER
Dear God, we pray for all leaders. We pray that they will do what You have called them to do. Protect us from those leaders who want to harm us. Give us the courage and wisdom to challenge unjust leadership. In Jesus' Name we pray. Amen.

DIGGING DEEPER:

God Didn't Say That! Reflections on False Prophecy in the Old Testament

No single test was good enough to authenticate the ministry of a real prophet. However, there are several defining characteristics. Among them are a clear call from God, a consciousness of their words being inspired by the Spirit of God, and speaking only in the name of the Lord.

Another mark of the true prophet was that he shunned professionalism. In other words, he did not prophesy for money. False prophets were often the paid servants of some higher authority. For example, Balak, the king of Moab, paid Balaam; the full account is given in Numbers 22. Amos flatly denied any professionalism. He spoke judgment on Amaziah, the priest of Bethel (vv. 10-13)

Then Amos answered and said to Amaziah, "I was no prophet, nor a prophet's son, but I

LESSON 7 • JULY 13, 2025

was a herdsman and a dresser of sycamore figs. But the LORD took me from following the flock and said to me, 'Go, prophesy to my people, Israel.' Therefore, hear the word of the LORD …" *(Amos 7:14b-16a).*

Unlike modern prosperity prophets, Micah says the false prophets prophesy for hire. They tell the people what they want to hear.

Thus says the LORD concerning the prophets who lead my people astray, who cry "Peace" when they have something to eat, but declare war against him who puts nothing into their mouths (Micah 3:5; cf. v. 6-7).

It is the duty/mandate of the prophet to speak to the people the word of the Lord, whether they want to hear it or not (cf. Ezekiel 33:6-7). From the people's perspective, the prophets are like gnats beside a still pond.

HOW TO SAY IT
Diviners. di-VIE-ners.
Equity. EH-kwi-tee.

DAILY HOME BIBLE READINGS

MONDAY
Do Not Pervert Justice
(Exodus 23:1–8)

TUESDAY
False Prophecies of Peace
(Ezekiel 13:15–20)

WEDNESDAY
Act in the Fear of the Lord
(2 Chronicles 19:4–10)

THURSDAY
Walk Blamelessly, Do Right, Speak Truth (Psalm 15)

FRIDAY
Known by Their Fruits
(Matthew 7:15–20)

SATURDAY
Woe to Those Striving with God
(Isaiah 45:5–13)

SUNDAY
Sold Out Religion
(Micah 3:5–12)

PREPARE FOR NEXT SUNDAY
Read **Micah 6:3–8** and study "Justice, Love, and Humility."

Sources:
Achtemeier, Paul J., ed. *The HarperCollins Bible Dictionary.* New York: HarperCollins Publishing, 1996. 680, 888.
Smith, Ralph L. *Micah–Malachi.* Word Biblical Commentary. Waco, TX: World Books Publishers, 1984. 32–34.
Waltke, Bruce K. *A Commentary on Micah.* Grand Rapids, MI: Eerdmans 2007. 181–183.

COMMENTS / NOTES:

LESSON 8 • JULY 20, 2025

JUSTICE, LOVE, AND HUMILITY

BIBLE BASIS: MICAH 6:3–8

BIBLE TRUTH: God instructs the unjust to be just, to love kindness, and to walk humbly with Him.

MEMORY VERSE: "He hath shewed thee, O man, what is good; and what doth the LORD require of thee, but to do justly, and to love mercy, and to walk humbly with thy God?" (Micah 6:8).

LESSON AIM: By the end of the lesson, your students will: KNOW how to honor God gratefully by exhibiting the character traits that God requires; EXPRESS feelings about living up to God's expectations for us to be just, loving, and humble; and LEAD the community into making God's requirements a reality.

BACKGROUND SCRIPTURE: Micah 6; Deuteronomy 10:12-22—Read and incorporate the insights gained from the Background Scriptures into your study of the lesson.

LESSON SCRIPTURE

MICAH 6:3–8, KJV

3 O my people, what have I done unto thee? and wherein have I wearied thee? testify against me.

4 For I brought thee up out of the land of Egypt, and redeemed thee out of the house of servants; and I sent before thee Moses, Aaron, and Miriam.

5 O my people, remember now what Balak king of Moab consulted, and what Balaam the son of Beor answered him from Shittim unto Gilgal; that ye may know the righteousness of the LORD.

6 Wherewith shall I come before the LORD, and bow myself before the high God? shall I come before him with burnt offerings, with calves of a year old?

7 Will the LORD be pleased with thousands of rams, or with ten thousands of rivers of oil? shall I give my firstborn for my transgression, the fruit of my body for the sin of my soul?

8 He hath shewed thee, O man, what is good; and what doth the LORD require of thee, but to do justly, and to love mercy, and to walk humbly with thy God?

BIBLICAL DEFINITIONS

A. Redeemed (Micah 6:4) *padah* (Heb.)—To ransom, rescue, or deliver.

B. Mercy (v. 8) *khesed* (Heb.)—Goodness or kindness (especially as extended to the lowly, needy, miserable, or in a lower position of power).

LIFE NEED FOR TODAY'S LESSON

AIM: Students will sometimes forget what a benefactor has done for them or they make insincere efforts to show gratitude.

INTRODUCTION
God's Court Case

Micah's prophecy begins with a general announcement to Samaria and Jerusalem that God has a case to present against the nations of Israel and Judah. He then lays out the first of two series of judgments against Israel and Judah. Micah describes the sins that they

LESSON 8 • JULY 20, 2025

have committed against God as well as their fellow man.

Israel has allowed the worship of idols and other gods to take root in their religious practices. Pagan practices have become a part of Israel's worship to Yahweh. For example, they have engaged in the pagan ritual of temple prostitution. They have presented the money earned by prostitutes to God as an offering (**Micah 1:7**; cf. **Deuteronomy 23:17–18**).

The wealthy have oppressed the poor to gain more wealth and power. They lie awake at night, devising how they will collect more land by defrauding others (**Micah 2:1–2**).

Israel's leaders have neglected their duties and led the people astray. Rather than protecting and instructing their citizens, they have exploited and misled them. Similarly, the prophets have chosen to seek after money, rather than speak God's truth to the people. They prophesy according to how much money their words might bring them. Israel's leaders are not directed by God; their actions are driven by greed and ambition (**Micah 3:11**).

Micah's first series of judgments is followed by a hopeful look to a distant future, when Israel will be restored. God will eventually redeem His exiled people once again. He will lift Israel up above all other nations.

It is against this backdrop that Micah's second series of judgments begins in chapter 6. This second series of judgments also concerns the issue of social justice in Israel.

BIBLE LEARNING
AIM: Students will understand that the Israelites' disrespect toward God and disobedience of God's commands arose from their lack of regard and gratitude for God's saving acts for them.

I. GOD REMINDS ISRAEL OF HIS BENEVOLENCE (MICAH 6:3–5)

Through the prophet Micah, God questions why Israel has turned against Him. Why have they turned to false gods? What did God do to deserve their indifference? He recounts how He delivered Israel from the slavery of Egypt. It would seem that Israel has forgotten the significance of their freedom from Egypt and His hand in delivering them. God has done nothing to provoke their negative attitude toward Him. He graciously rescued them from a life of cruel slavery, and provided leaders to guide them.

Clarifying the Issues (verses 3–5)
3 O my people, what have I done unto thee? and wherein have I wearied thee? testify against me.

Here the Lord pleads His case. He asks the people of Judah the reason they have become so unfaithful as His covenant people. Specifically, He asks what He has done to them and how He has wearied (Heb. *la'ah*, **la-AH**) them. This word means to be tired or to give up. The Lord asks, "How have I offended you? How could you become dissatisfied with me?" He gives them an opportunity to testify (Heb. *'anah*, **ah-NAH**, literally to answer or, in a legal suit, to provide opposing testimony) against Him.

4 For I brought thee up out of the land of Egypt, and redeemed thee out of the house of servants; and I sent before thee Moses, Aaron, and Miriam.

Next the Lord rehearses His blessings and how gracious He has been toward His people. He brought them out of Egypt. He redeemed them from slavery. He sent Moses, Aaron, and Miriam. They were not left without leaders, but were guided to the Promised Land.

5 O my people, remember now what Balak king of Moab consulted, and what

LESSON 8 • JULY 20, 2025

Balaam the son of Beor answered him from Shittim unto Gilgal; that ye may know the righteousness of the LORD.

Next the Lord brings up the incident with Balak the King of Moab and Balaam the prophet. Balak feared the Israelites coming out of Egypt, so he hired Balaam to pronounce a curse on them (**Numbers 22:1-6**). Quite the opposite happened, as the Lord caused a donkey to speak to Balaam and refuse to go any further (**Numbers 22:22-30**). This opened Balaam's eyes to an angel of the Lord in the middle of the road, who told him not to follow through with the king's orders (**Numbers 22:31-35**). After this, Balaam could do nothing but bless them. Each time he opened his mouth, he blessed God's people. The Lord here shows them that even when their enemies tried to curse them, God fulfilled His promise and they were blessed instead.

Shittim and Gilgal are references to the Israelites' conquest of the land. Shittim was the place where Joshua camped east of the Jordan River, and Gilgal is where they crossed to take over the land. It was quite common in military annals of the ancient Near East to summarize the itinerary of the conquering king as a way to summarize the whole conquest. The reference to these places was God's way of reminding them of all that He had done to give them the land they now enjoyed.

QUESTION 1
Why do you think Israel had forgotten the significance of their miraculous deliverance from Egyptian slavery (**Micah 6:4**)?

II. GOD REQUIRES JUSTICE, LOVE, AND HUMILITY (vv. 6-8)

What can Israel do to correct their broken relationship with God? Their immediate response is to offer sacrifices to God. They first suggest reasonable sacrifices of calves and burnt offerings. However, they exponentially increase their offer of sacrifice to ridiculous levels. They ultimately offer the human sacrifice of a firstborn child, which was customary of pagan sacrifice but prohibited by the covenant law (**Leviticus 18:21, 20:2-5**). The ridiculous nature of their offers seems to imply that there might be no pleasing Yahweh. However, Micah's prophecy, in keeping with other Israelite prophecies, clearly indicates that the inward condition of one's heart is of more concern to God than outward religiosity.

Honor and Respect God (verses 6-8)

6 Wherewith shall I come before the Lord, and bow myself before the High God? Shall I come before him with burnt offerings, with calves of a year old?

Micah establishes a courtroom setting in which the Lord is the accuser (plaintiff) who charges Israel, the accused (defendant), with social and religious injustice. Judah attempts to respond to God's indictment by asking how they can approach God, who is so high and mighty under the shadow of their own sin and transgressions.

The people of Judah acknowledge the royal and lofty nature of God and realize that the King of kings is worthy to receive their obeisance. Because of the greed of the religious and political leadership, they have not paid God the respect and honor He deserves.

Not only does God deserve their honor as the King of kings, He must be offered sacrifices, particularly burnt offerings. The burnt offering (Heb. *'olah*, **oh-LAH**) is a gift that ascends to the heavens. A portion is given to the priest to offer to God and the remainder is consumed or burned. The offering is dedicated completely to God. Young calves, or any animal less than a year old, were often sacrificed to render this type of offering. By their question, Judah knows they should have been engaging in these sacrifices. Yet their questions also indicate how far they have strayed from the Lord's covenant promise.

7 Will the LORD be pleased with thousands of rams, or with ten thousands of rivers of oil? shall I give my first-born for my transgression, the fruit of my body for the sin of my soul?

Judah continues an arrogant defense of their crimes by sarcastically asking what the Lord requires. The people know that sacrifices of rams are pleasing to the Lord. Yet they exaggerate how many sacrifices they should give to God by asking if thousands of rams will do. The Hebrews are aware that oil is used in anointing royalty and in presenting gifts to God. Yet they are overzealous in their need to repent and ask if many rivers, not vials, of oil will suffice. Micah again uses this rhetorical line of reasoning to show how far the people are removed from God. They are not aware repentance needs to occur.

The line of questioning and sarcasm continues with Judah even offering their firstborn as restitution for sin. Micah alludes to the importance of the Lord receiving the firstfruits of the harvest for sacrifice. This passage also alludes to God delivering the firstborn of the Hebrew children from the angel of death during Israel's enslavement in Egypt (**Exodus 12**). This giving of the firstborn also refers to human sacrifices practiced in Judah under kings Ahaz (**2 Kings 16:3**) and Manasseh (**2 Kings 21:6**).

8 He hath shown thee, O man, what is good; and what doth the LORD require of thee, but to do justly, and to love mercy, and to walk humbly with thy God?

Micah now offers a response to the questions of **verses 6 and 7**. None of what Judah has offered is what the Lord desires. God does not seek sacrifices, offerings, or rituals. The Lord wants the people to treat each other fairly and to walk according to His way. Obedience is better than sacrifice (**1 Samuel 15:22**).

To do justly or carry out justice comes from the Hebrew word *mishpat* (**mish-PAWT**). It means judgment or a right sentence. It is the establishment of right through fair and legal procedures in accordance with the will of God. Mercy is translated from the Hebrew word *chesed* (**KHEH-sed**, pity, loving kindness, or doing good for those in a lower position) and is similar to the New Testament concept of grace. The idea of walking humbly with God is juxtaposed with Judah's arrogance and refusal to lean on the Lord (**Micah 3:11**). Because the people have allowed their lust for money to interfere with their relationship with God and have chosen their own selfish gain, Micah warns that He wants them to submit, to return to the commandments and the way of the Lord.

QUESTION 2
Why do you think their first response was outward sacrifice, rather than inward change (**vv. 6–7**)?

BIBLE APPLICATION
AIM: Students will understand that because of all that God has done for them, they must live upright lives to show their gratitude to Him.

We live in a world where we are bombarded with advertisements daily. It has been said that the average person today sees more ads in a day than someone in the 1950s saw in their lifetime. These ads have a subtle way of making us ungrateful and dissatisfied, so we crave new products and luxuries and pursue them no matter what the cost—even injustice. God wants us to be satisfied with the blessings He has given us. By remembering what God has already done for us and who He is, we will be motivated to seek justice for others, not wealth and comfort for ourselves.

STUDENTS' RESPONSES

AIM: Students will recognize that true worship of God goes beyond the performance of ritual.

Consider the ways that God has blessed you. Do you sometimes forget all that He has done in your life? In order to get out of yourself this week and focus on God, create a list of things that God has done for you. As you create this list, think about one thing that you can do for others who are treated unjustly.

PRAYER

God, we want to walk in Your justice, and live our lives in love and mercy with one another. Thank You for first loving us and caring for us even when do not follow Your ways of justice. In Jesus' Name we pray. Amen.

Digging Deeper:
God is Suing His People?
God Brings a Lawsuit

The prophets often used various forms of speech to forcefully communicate God's message. One example is the covenant lawsuit (Hebrew: *riv*). To portray the seriousness of the charges against them, the prophet would portray the Lord as bringing a lawsuit against his own people. Accordingly, God is seen as the plaintiff, the prosecuting attorney, the judge, and the executor of the judgment. An example is provided in Isaiah 3.

- God as the judge

The Lord has taken his place to contend; he stands to judge peoples (v. 13).

- The defendants

The Lord will enter into judgment with the elders and princes of his people (v. 14a).

- The charges

"It is you who have devoured the vineyard, the spoil of the poor is in your house. What do you mean by crushing my people, by grinding the face of the poor?" declares the Lord God of hosts. The Lord said: "Because the daughters of Zion are haughty and walk with outstretched necks, glancing wantonly with their eyes, mincing along as they go, tinkling with their feet ..." (vv. 14b-16).

- Judgment

Therefore, the Lord will (vv. 17-26)

In Micah 6, God acts as judge (v. 1) and calls for the mountains to serve as the witnesses (vv. 1b-2). The picture is one of God putting his people on the witness stand and interrogating them.

O my people, what have I done to you? How have I wearied you? Answer me! For I brought you up from the land of Egypt and redeemed you from the house of slavery, and I sent before you Moses, Aaron, and Miriam. O my people, remember what Balak king of Moab devised, and what Balaam the son of Beor answered him, and what happened from Shittim to Gilgal, that you may know the righteous acts of the Lord (Micah 6:3-5).

HOW TO SAY IT

Shittim. shee-**TEEM**.
Beor. be-**OR**.

LESSON 8 • JULY 20, 2025

DAILY HOME BIBLE READINGS

MONDAY
What Does the Lord Require?
(Deuteronomy 10:12–22)

TUESDAY
Who Gives Speech to Mortals?
(Exodus 4:10–17)

WEDNESDAY
The Word the Lord Speaks
(Numbers 22:1–14)

THURSDAY
Do Only What I Tell You
(Numbers 22:15–21)

FRIDAY
Speak Only What I Tell You
(Numbers 22:31–38)

SATURDAY
You Have Blessed My Enemies
(Numbers 23:1–12)

SUNDAY
Justice, Kindness, and Humility
(Micah 6:3–8)

PREPARE FOR NEXT SUNDAY

Read **Micah 7:14–20** and study "God Shows Clemency."

Sources:
Brown, Francis, S. R. Driver, and Charles Briggs. *The Brown-Driver-Briggs Hebrew and English Lexicon.* Peabody, MA: Hendrickson Publishers, 2007. S.vv. "Chesed" and "Padah."
Burge, Gary M. and Andrew E. Hill, eds. *Baker Illustrated Bible Commentary.* Grand Rapids, MI: Baker Books, 2012. 860–870.
Butler, Trent C., ed. "Balaam." *Holman Bible Dictionary.* Electronic Edition, Quickverse. Nashville, TN: Holman Bible Publishers, 1991.
Carson, D. A., R. T. France, J. A. Motyer, G. J. Wenham, eds. *New Bible Commentary.* Downer's Grove, IL: Intervarsity Press, 1994. 830.
Easton, M. G. "Balaam." *Easton's Bible Dictionary.* 1st ed. Oklahoma City, OK: Ellis Enterprises, 1993.
Hill, Andrew E. and John H. Walton. *A Survey of the Old Testament.* Grand Rapids, MI: Zondervan. 2009. 642–647.
Keck, Leander, ed. *The Twelve Prophets.* The New Interpreter's Bible. Vol. 7. Nashville, TN: Abingdon Press, 1996. 533–534, 577–580.
Orr, James, ed. "Balaam." *International Standard Bible Encyclopedia.* Electronic Edition. Omaha, NE: Quickverse, 1998.

COMMENTS / NOTES:

LESSON 9 • JULY 27, 2025

GOD SHOWS CLEMENCY

BIBLE BASIS: MICAH 7:14–20

BIBLE TRUTH: God will show compassion and faithfulness to His people, even to the unjust.

MEMORY VERSE: "Where is another God like you, who pardons the guilt of the remnant, overlooking the sins of his special people? You will not stay angry with your people forever, because you delight in showing unfailing love" (Micah 7:18).

LESSON AIM: By the end of the lesson, your students will: LEARN of God's mercy even when punishment seems in order; REFLECT on experiences when God's mercy and compassion were more than expected; and CARRY OUT acts of mercy and compassion.

BACKGROUND SCRIPTURE: Micah 7:11–20; Psalm 13—Read and incorporate the insights gained from the Background Scriptures into your study of the lesson.

LESSON SCRIPTURE

MICAH 7:14–20, KJV

14 Feed thy people with thy rod, the flock of thine heritage, which dwell solitarily in the wood, in the midst of Carmel: let them feed in Bashan and Gilead, as in the days of old.

15 According to the days of thy coming out of the land of Egypt will I shew unto him marvellous things.

16 The nations shall see and be confounded at all their might: they shall lay their hand upon their mouth, their ears shall be deaf.

17 They shall lick the dust like a serpent, they shall move out of their holes like worms of the earth: they shall be afraid of the LORD our God, and shall fear because of thee.

18 Who is a God like unto thee, that pardoneth iniquity, and passeth by the transgression of the remnant of his heritage? he retaineth not his anger for ever, because he delighteth in mercy.

19 He will turn again, he will have compassion upon us; he will subdue our iniquities; and thou wilt cast all their sins into the depths of the sea.

20 Thou wilt perform the truth to Jacob, and the mercy to Abraham, which thou hast sworn unto our fathers from the days of old.

BIBLICAL DEFINITIONS

A. Iniquity (Micah 7:18) *'avon* (Heb.)— Perversity or guilt.

B. Remnant (v. 18) *she'erit* (Heb.)— The rest, what is left, remaining descendants.

LIFE NEED FOR TODAY'S LESSON

AIM: Students will discover that evil and injustice are not met with corrective justice, but are trumped by mercy.

INTRODUCTION

God's Mercy for His People

Micah speaks a psalm of trust and salvation for Israel. He lets them know that the Lord will not let their enemies gloat over them. This is probably a prophecy of the fall of Jerusalem in 586 B.C. Additionally, he informs them that one day their walls will be rebuilt and

LESSON 9 • JULY 27, 2025

foreigners from Assyria to Egypt will come to be part of Israel. At the same time, the rest of the nations will be uninhabited as punishment for what they did to God's people. This leads Micah to speak of God's mercy and faithfulness to His people.

BIBLE LEARNING
AIM: Students will describe the uniqueness of the Lord, who among all gods forgives sin.

I. THE LORD IS MY SHEPHERD (MICAH 7:14–15)

Micah is asking God to care for His people in the same tender and affectionate manner that a shepherd oversees his flock. More specifically, He requests divine provision because they are God's children. He uses the imagery of lush pastures in Gilead and Bashan to further urge God to restore not only the people, but the land.

God Cares for the People (verses 14–15)

14 Feed thy people with thy rod, the flock of thine heritage, which dwell solitarily in the wood, in the midst of Carmel: let them feed in Bashan and Gilead, as in the days of old.

Starting with the relational image of a shepherd, Micah prays for the fulfillment of the promised salvation and restoration of vv. 11–13 (**v. 14**). The prayer is reminiscent of Psalm 23:4, where David portrays the Lord as a Shepherd, who with loving care, leads His sheep with the rod and the staff. The people of God are called the flock of His inheritance or possession. They belong to Him (**cf. v. 18; Psalms 94:14, 100:3**). But Israel was dwelling solitarily in the field. Dwelling "solitarily in the woods" is probably used to stress that they were not living in a good situation. Not only is their ground poor, but they are also cut off from other peoples and cannot get goods or help from them. So, Micah prays that their Shepherd will once again let them feed in Bashan and Gilead, cities that had proverbially fruitful pasturelands. This may also have been a prayer for the return of that rich and fertile land to the people of Zion (**Zechariah 10:10**).

15 According to the days of thy coming out of the land of Egypt will I shew unto him marvellous things.

God gives an answer to the prophet's prayer. He will protect, save, defend, and work miracles for them in their restoration, such as He did for their fathers in their return from Egypt to the Promised Land. God showed them His wonders then, and He will do it again. His future acts for them will include similar displays of His redemptive grace and power on their behalf. With the restoration of Israel, Micah anticipated manifestations of God's power and leadership like those at the Red Sea, Sinai, and other cities along the Exodus out of Egypt.

QUESTION 1
What is the writer comparing God's people to in **verse 14**?

II. EMBARRASSMENT (vv. 16–17)

After Micah requests favor for Israel, he then asks God to punish their enemies by shaming them and having them acknowledge the limitations of their power compared to the Lord. Micah is very specific when he relays to God the wrath he wants them to receive. Micah's petition is for all of their enemies to experience God in such a way that His dominance and authority cannot be doubted or disputed.

The Awesomeness of God's Power (verses 16–17)

16 The nations shall see and be confounded at all their might: they shall lay their hand upon their mouth, their ears shall be deaf.

When the Lord begins to work miracles for His people again, His activity will have a dramatic effect on the nations around them, just as it did on the Egyptians at the time of the Exodus. They will see this and be confounded in spite of all their might, because when they see the mighty acts of God, they will realize how weak they really are. The nations, who thought they were so strong, will realize that their strength is nothing compared to God's power, and they will be ashamed of their strength instead of proud. They will be so dismayed that they can neither speak nor hear. They will lay their hands on their mouths in awe and amazement. Their ears will become deaf, perhaps meaning that they will turn a deaf ear to all this; they do not want to hear anything more about the Lord's powerful redemptive acts for His people.

17 They shall lick the dust like a serpent, they shall move out of their holes like worms of the earth: they shall be afraid of the LORD our God, and shall fear because of thee.

Micah continues with his description of the heathen nations' reaction to the Lord's miracles, and again uses symbolic actions. "They shall lick the dust like a serpent, they shall move out of their holes like worms of the earth" are two parallel lines expressing a single idea. It is a graphic way to show the humiliation of the nations, and lying with their faces in the dust (like snakes) shows how weak and lowly they are. The expression "lick dust like a snake" may have **Genesis 3:14** as its background and may also be compared to the modern idiom "to bite the dust," symbolizing death in defeat (cf. **Psalm 72:9**). Finally the nations will come trembling out of their hiding places, and they will turn in fear to the Lord and will be afraid of him.

III. WHO IS LIKE GOD? (vv. 18–20)

How fitting is it that Micah would begin to praise God? He recognizes that there is no being on Earth or in heaven as merciful as God, and begins praising Him. After considering the nation's immorality in comparison to God's grace, Micah boasts of the love and compassion God repeatedly extends through His never-ending forgiveness.

God Delights in Mercy (verses 18–20)

18 Who is a God like unto thee, that pardoneth iniquity, and passeth by the transgression of the remnant of his heritage? he retaineth not his anger for ever, because he delighteth in mercy.

Verse 18 opens with a rhetorical question, "Who is a God like unto thee …?" The answer expected is clearly that there is no one like God. The question here is a way of affirming God's incomparability, particularly in His forgiving love and grace. The characteristic that sets Him apart is His ability and willingness to forgive sin. God's forgiveness "that pardoneth iniquity" is suitable to His greatness. It is not like the imperfect forgiveness that people offer, but instead full, free, bottomless, boundless, and absolute. The magnitude of God's forgiveness is underscored by the use of three different, common words in this verse and the next for sin ("iniquity" and "transgression" in **verse 18**, and "iniquities" and "sins" in **verse 19**), their purpose and effect are to emphasize the completeness of God's ability to forgive all kinds of sin.

God does not retain His anger forever. He may be angry with His people when they sin, but once they have repented or been punished, He instead takes pleasure in showing mercy. He is more ready to save than to destroy. Nothing can please Him better

LESSON 9 • JULY 27, 2025

than having the opportunity to show mercy to the sinner.

19 He will turn again, he will have compassion upon us; he will subdue our iniquities; and thou wilt cast all their sins into the depths of the sea. 20 Thou wilt perform the truth to Jacob, and the mercy to Abraham, which thou hast sworn unto our fathers from the days of old.

Because He is such a God as described in verse 18, "he will turn again." His face has been long turned from His people because of their sins. But He will have compassion on them, pitying our state and feeling for our sorrows. He will defeat the iniquities of His people, and demonstrate His complete victory over their sin. Though they have been mighty, He will bring them down. The theme recalls the treatment of their enemies in verse 10. To further accentuate the extent of His forgiveness, He will cast all their sins into the depths of the sea—He will fully pardon them. The word "compassion" suggests a tender, maternal love. The word "subdue" paints the picture of sin as an enemy that God conquers and liberates His people from (**cf. Romans 6:14**). God overcomes sin and sets His people free.

The book of Micah, despite its threats of punishment and judgment in the earlier chapters, ends on a note of joy and confidence that the nation will eventually enjoy a restored relationship with the Lord. In concluding his prophecy, Micah sees God's future work as a continuation of His covenants and promises to the Israelites' ancestors. He knew that the same love, compassion, and mercy He showed to their parents was available to them, if they received it in faith. Regardless of the moral and spiritual decline of His people, God can be relied on to be faithful to His covenant promises.

QUESTION 2
What does God take delight in doing (**Micah 7:18**)?

BIBLE APPLICATION
AIM: Students will believe that God's forgiveness is unconditional. God forgives completely.

Just like chivalry, some may say that compassion is a thing of the past. While this may appear true at first glance, innumerable examples of empathy, forgiveness, and reconciliation suggest otherwise. Every day we face situations where we can turn the other cheek and extend compassion, or subject someone to the consequences of their actions. In the same way, although God demands justice, He also has mercy for those who repent. This is fully demonstrated by Jesus' work on the Cross.

STUDENTS' RESPONSES
AIM: Students will praise God because of His mercy.

Think of a specific person you know who has done something wrong. Should that person receive mercy or punishment? Make a point to offer forgiveness for this person, and if possible, alleviate the consequences of their actions.

PRAYER
Lord, we do not always want to forgive, but we know that You forgive us. We serve a God who knows that we are sometimes slow to accept forgiveness or give forgiveness to others. Take care of us and our hearts that we may always do what is right and pleasing before You. In Jesus' Name we pray. Amen.

DIGGING DEEPER:

It's All Wrong – A Survey of Sin Word in the Old Testament

Micah 7:18-19 uses three different words to

describe sin, each with its own nuances. They are worth examining.

Micah asked the rhetorical question, *"Who is a God like you, pardoning **iniquity** ...?"* The Hebrew word translated iniquity is *avon*. It means to be bent, crooked, or twisted. It connotes the idea of that which twists out of God's straight way. So, what is described here is not a defect of the intelligence, but of the will. The Bible says that we lack the will power to do what we know is right. The good news is that God forgives iniquity (Psalm 32:5).

Continuing, Micah asked, *"Who is a God like you, pardoning iniquity and passing over **transgression** ...?"* The Hebrew word translated transgression is *pesha*. It refers to rebellion. It means to revolt or refuse to submit to authority. Hence the idea is rebellion against God. These people want to assert their own authority or ego and defy God and his authority. This was the sin of Adam and thus all humans are guilty of transgression. *Pesha* is used repeatedly in Amos to describe crimes against God (Amos 1:3, 6, 9, 11, 13; 2:1, 4, 6; 3:14; 4:4; 5:12). The good news of the gospel is that Jesus makes intercession for transgressors (Isa 53:12).

Finally, Micah declares, *"You will cast all our **sins** into the depths of the sea."* The Hebrew words translated sin is *chet*. It is a term drawn from archery; it means to miss the mark or the bullseye. Among the people of Benjamin were 700 chosen left-handed men who could sling a stone at a hair and not miss (i.e., sin; Judges 20:16). *Chet* was done out of ignorance; it's a failing to measure up to the standard. The first time the word is used is in the narrative of Cain and Abel, where *chet* is likened to a wild animal lying in wait to devour him. Again, the good news is that the death and resurrection of Jesus deals with the problem of sin and therefore can be forgiven.

HOW TO SAY IT

Solitarily.	so-li-**TA**-ri-lee.
Pardoneth.	**PAR**-dun-ith.
Retaineth.	ree-**TAYN**-ith.

DAILY HOME BIBLE READINGS

MONDAY
I Trusted in Your Steadfast Love
(Psalm 13)

TUESDAY
My Sheep Were Scattered
(Ezekiel 34:1–6)

WEDNESDAY
The Lord Will Shepherd His Sheep
(Ezekiel 34:7–16)

THURSDAY
You are My Sheep
(Ezekiel 34:23–31)

FRIDAY
Troubling Times of Woe
(Micah 7:1–6)

SATURDAY
I Will Look to the Lord
(Micah 7:7–11)

SUNDAY
God Delights in Showing Clemency
(Micah 7:14–20)

PREPARE FOR NEXT SUNDAY

Read **Isaiah 59:15b–21** and study "Our Redeemer Comes."

Sources:

Achtemeier, Paul J., ed. *The HarperCollins Bible Dictionary.* New York: HarperCollins Publishing, 1996. 919, 923, 1026.

Allen, Leslie C. *The Books of Joel, Obadiah, Jonah and Micah.* New International Commentary of the Old Testament. Grand Rapids, MI: Wm. B. Eerdmans, 1976.

Barker, Kenneth L. *Micah, Nahum, Habakkuk, Zephaniah.* The New American Commentary. Vo. 20. Nashville, TN: Broadman & Holman Publishers, 1999.

LESSON 9 • JULY 27, 2025

Boice, J. M. *The Minor Prophets*. Complete in one edition, 2 volumes. Grand Rapids, MI: Kregel, 1996. S.v. 2:24.

Clark, David J. and Norm Mundhenk. *A Translator's Handbook on the Book of Micah*, UBS Handbook Series. London: United Bible Societies, 1982.

Craigie, P. C. *Twelve Prophets*. 2 vols. Philadelphia: Westminster, 1985. 2:19. Smith, Ralph L. *Micah–Malachi*. Word Biblical Commentary. Vol. 32. Dallas: Word Books Publishers, Inc., 1984. 58–59.

Wolfendale, James. "Minor Prophets." *The Preacher's Homiletical Commentary*. New York: Funk and Wagnalls, 1892.

Waltke, Bruce K. *A Commentary on Micah*. Grand Rapids, MI: Eerdmans 2007. 181-183.

COMMENTS / NOTES:

LESSON 10 • AUGUST 3, 2025

OUR REDEEMER COMES

BIBLE BASIS: ISAIAH 59:15b–21

BIBLE TRUTH: Isaiah and the psalmist promise a time when God will come as a Redeemer with a foundation of righteousness and justice and will place God's spirit on those who repent of their sins.

MEMORY VERSE: "And the Redeemer shall come to Zion, and unto them that turn from transgression in Jacob, saith the LORD" (Isaiah 59:20).

LESSON AIM: By the end of the lesson, your students will: EXPLORE how God promises a renewed covenant relationship; REVEAL their feelings about the cruelty and violence of society; and EXPRESS gratitude and joy for God's salvation from worldly dangers and work toward a renewed community.

BACKGROUND SCRIPTURE: Isaiah 59:15–21; Psalm 89:11–18; Exodus 6:2–8— Read and incorporate the insights gained from the Background Scriptures into your study of the lesson.

LESSON SCRIPTURE

ISAIAH 59:15b–21, KJV

15b The LORD saw it, and it displeased him that there was no judgment.

16 And he saw that there was no man, and wondered that there was no intercessor: therefore his arm brought salvation unto him; and his righteousness, it sustained him.

17 For he put on righteousness as a breastplate, and an helmet of salvation upon his head; and he put on the garments of vengeance for clothing, and was clad with zeal as a cloak.

18 According to their deeds, accordingly he will repay, fury to his adversaries, recompence to his enemies; to the islands he will repay recompence.

19 So shall they fear the name of the LORD from the west, and his glory from the rising of the sun. When the enemy shall come in like a flood, the Spirit of the LORD shall lift up a standard against him.

20 And the Redeemer shall come to Zion, and unto them that turn from transgression in Jacob, saith the LORD.

21 As for me, this is my covenant with them, saith the LORD; My spirit that is upon thee, and my words which I have put in thy mouth, shall not depart out of thy mouth, nor out of the mouth of thy seed, nor out of the mouth of thy seed's seed, saith the LORD, from henceforth and forever.

BIBLICAL DEFINITIONS

A. Intercessor (Isaiah 59:16) *paga'* (Heb.)—One who intervenes or interposes oneself.

B. Recompence (v. 18) *gemul* (Heb.)—Punishment or reward to someone for an action; benefit.

LIFE NEED FOR TODAY'S LESSON

AIM: Students will know that there are times when everything around us seems violent, cruel, and immoral.

INTRODUCTION

God's Vision for Isaiah

The events that were transpiring around him inspired Isaiah to give His prophe-

LESSON 10 • AUGUST 3, 2025

cies during a crucial time in the history of Judah. In approximately 791 B.C., Uzziah became king of Judah. Forty years into his reign, he was stricken with leprosy, so his son Jotham became co-regent, helping him rule. Around 745 B.C., Assyria, a dominant and opposing empire, began to shift their focus in an attempt to conquer the Mediterranean area, including Judah and many other nations. In the year that King Uzziah died, Jotham began to rule alone and Isaiah had one of his greatest visions.

BIBLE LEARNING

AIM: Students will praise God and know that the Lord will not be angry with the chosen people forever.

I. INTERCESSION (Isaiah 59:15b–16)

The writer discloses that there was a paradigm shift in the land. His report reveals that the people abandoned truth and embraced wickedness because harsh retaliation was the consequence for siding with righteousness. The historical truth is that people were physically persecuted and even killed for following the Lord. However, this is not a foreign or antiquated premise because even today, people suffer and die for righteousness in countries like China and Syria.

Abandoned Truth (verses 15b–16)

15b The LORD saw it, and it displeased him that there was no judgment. 16 And he saw that there was no man, and wondered that there was no intercessor: therefore his arm brought salvation unto him; and his righteousness, it sustained him.

These verses portray the social degradation of the people of God. They directly follow **verses 14–15a**, where we see the consequence of what happens when people live in lies and assume that it is alright to oppress those who are weaker, neglect God, and turn away from His commandments and the path of righteousness. First, "truth faileth," which means that truth has been left behind or abandoned. People do not care for the truth but tell lies with impunity. Although not limited to politicians, people say the lies over and over until they are somehow convinced that the lies are truth. Second, whoever turns away from sin is considered out of sorts or insane. One would expect that everyone departing from evil would feel not hatred and censure, but commendation and appreciation. Unfortunately, this is not the case; on the contrary, the person who takes this step will "make himself a prey." In a society that is increasingly morally bankrupt, turning aside from evil could easily make one seem the most apparent loser. Third, there was injustice—that is, no social justice, no sense of the "right" manifestly ruling in the common relations of life.

God sees the helplessness of His people and cares about it. The word "intercessor," from the Hebrew root word pagaʽ (**pah-GAH**), which also occurred in **53:12,** means to cover the breach with one's body. In the same manner as in **Isaiah 53**, God has to intervene on behalf of His people. God looked down and saw the degenerate and hopeless condition of His people. He knew how far the evil spread, until the whole people were corrupted. To make matters worse, God saw no one stood for truth and righteousness—none such as Abraham, Moses, or Phinehas (**Genesis 15:6; Exodus 33:11–14; Numbers 25:7–8**). That God wondered does not suggest a surprise or ignorance of the situation, but rather astonishment. As no human intercessor could be found among the exiles, God Himself brought salvation. He was patient and waited for a disobedient Israel to turn to Him. He waited and longed for a man to lead them back to Him, but none defended His cause or proclaimed His truth, so the Lord did it Himself. If an intercessor had stepped forth, it would have saved Israel a lot of calamity, but the lack of an intercessor did not derail God's plan. His work would still go forth if none arose (cf. **Esther 4:14**). The Lord put on His armor and went forth to destroy His enemies, protect His people, and glorify His name.

II. GOD'S WRATH (vv. 17–21)

God's intervention will not be diplomatic; Judah's adversaries will know God's wrath and fury. Here we get our first glimpse of the armor of God. Paul tells his readers that they should guard themselves by donning this holy battle gear (**Ephesians 6:10–18**), but in this text it is used as a metaphor to describe the intensity with which God will admonish the enemy. It is no surprise that Isaiah uses warrior metaphors to describe God; He was often known as a battle-ax, conqueror, and divine warrior to the people of Israel, and they were confident that He would intervene on their behalf.

God's Armor (verses 17–21)

17 For he put on righteousness as a breastplate, and an helmet of salvation upon his head; and he put on the garments of vengeance for clothing, and was clad with zeal as a cloak.

Using metaphorical language, Isaiah continues showing how the Lord will help His people. God appears as a man of war and puts on His arms—righteousness as breastplate, helmet and garments of salvation, and zeal as a cloak. The imagery is a prototype of **Ephesians 6:13–17**, where Paul exhorts his hearers to prepare for spiritual battle. The absence of offensive weapons such as bows or spears is striking; perhaps all God needs to execute vengeance on His enemies is His mighty arm. He will proceed in righting the wrongs and avenging the injuries of His people. Both in saving them and destroying their enemies, He will secure the honor of His faithfulness and justice, and by preserving His people, He maintains the honor and glory of His name. Since the heart and inward parts are protected by the breastplate, He calls righteousness His breastplate, to show the justness of His cause and His faithfulness in making good on His promises. In putting on the garments of vengeance, He is determined to punish His and His people's enemies. In this verse, God comes to the defense of His people.

18 According to their deeds, accordingly he will repay, fury to his adversaries, recompence to his enemies; to the islands he will repay recompence.

The Lord will deal with the enemies of His people according to the laws of retribution and retaliation. God will judge and repay His foes; He will execute vengeance on all those who have opposed Him. Sin's havoc on creation will be fully and richly repaid. Nothing will be left unrequited.

19 So shall they fear the name of the LORD from the west, and his glory from the rising of the sun. When the enemy shall come in like a flood, the Spirit of the LORD shall lift up a standard against him.

The negative picture gives way to positive results. The verse begins with a general statement that people from all over the world will fear the Lord. Here "fear" is understood as godly, reverent, childlike fear from the acknowledgement of His name. The last part of the verse gives further reasons for the reverential awe displayed toward the Lord—whenever the enemy comes to attack God's people, the Lord Himself raises a standard, showing that He is in control of the situation. No enemy can conquer God's people because He is ever-present to both demonstrate His care for His people and show His sovereignty. For this reason, people from across the world will fear the name of the Lord. God's name is His reputation and character; to fear His name is to fear Him, as He has revealed Himself in His acts on earth (**Psalm 86:11**). In the Scriptures, fear has both negative and positive connotations. Those who oppose the power and holiness of God have every reason to be afraid because He will judge them and consume them; on the other hand, those who know and revere Him enjoy the benefits of a personal relationship.

20 And he the Redeemer shall come to Zion, and unto them that turn from transgression in Jacob, saith the LORD. 21 As for me, this is my covenant with them, saith the LORD; My spirit that is upon thee, and my words which I have put in thy mouth, shall not depart out of thy mouth, nor out of the mouth of thy seed, nor out of the mouth of thy seed's seed, saith the LORD, from henceforth and for ever.

Verses 15–19 provided a description of how the Lord deals with the enemies of His people. He will be stern and just. There is a marked shift in tone in **verse 20**. Now He describes how differently He will deal with His own people and the generations that follow. First, God, acting as the Redeemer, shall come to Zion, but only to those who turn and repent from their sins. As such, turning from sin is the entry point into the covenant. God's judgment on His people was a foreshadowing of that final Day of the Lord, when all the nations will be judged. When it is ended, then "the Redeemer shall come to Zion" and the glorious kingdom will be established. Israel will be God's chosen and purified people, and the glory of the Lord will radiate from Mt. Zion. God's dealings are based on the covenant, which embodies the mercies that he has repeatedly promised to them. The substance of the covenant is encapsulated in two words— spirit and words. The words here may be the Torah. Israel will become a people that truly meditate on the Torah day and night. Both the words and the spirit belong together and constitute testimony that characterizes God's people not only in its momentary fulfillment but "from henceforth and for ever." The people of God must continue to embrace the Word by constantly hearing, saying, and learning it. They also have the responsibility to teach the word to their "seeds" and their "seeds' seeds," that is, to their children and grandchildren, as in the case of Timothy (cf. **2 Timothy 1:5**).

QUESTIONS 1 and 2

What is the purpose of the Lord putting on armor and robes of vengeance (**Isaiah 59:17**)?

What did God promise would not depart out of their mouth and why is this important (**v. 21**)?

BIBLE APPLICATION
AIM: Students will understand that disobedience causes God pain.

Morals and socioeconomic perspectives are two of the primary contributors to ideas of justice. Apart from individual premises of justice, nations have a prevailing interpretation of justice that shapes policy, governance, and culture. Justice does not solely address law; it addresses moral questions of right and wrong in humanity. Words such as accountability, equity, access, representation, and opportunity are key when analyzing justice in a society.

STUDENTS' RESPONSES
AIM: Students will praise God for His mercy and forgiveness.

Israel was to be very diligent in sharing their experiences with God with their children.

Isaiah 59:21 says, "[The words I have given you] will be on your lips and on the lips of your children and your children's children forever" (NLT). For this to happen, there must be an exchange of information from one generation to the next. Share your spiritual encounters and experiences in seeking justice with your children or others in the neighborhood. Not only will they know God through their personal experience, but they will know God through yours as well.

PRAYER

God, Your truth and love are amazing. We need to walk in Your truth and care for justice with passion and deliverance in our lives. Bless us and keep us. In Jesus' name we pray. Amen.

DIGGING DEEPER:
I Know Who Called Me

The prophets have several defining characteristics. For example, every prophet (Hebrew: *navi*) is aware of a clear call (Hebrew: *navu*) from God. These call narratives are often included at the beginning of their oracles (Isaiah 6; Jeremiah 1; Ezekiel 1-3; Hosea 1:2; Jonah 1:1). A typical example is the call of Moses. God calls him to go and bring the people of Israel out of Egypt (vv. 1-12). However, Moses shows great reluctance and gives multiple excuses why God should choose someone else (vv. 13-7). But God reassures him that He will be with him, and Moses accepts. Note that God took the initiative in making a prophet. God always equipped the prophet to do the task.

Because the prophet knew God called him, the prophet was also conscious of his words being inspired by the Spirit of God. Hence the repeated use of the phrase, "Thus says the LORD ..." In essence, the prophet is an extension of God's personality. Therefore, the prophet must preach.

When Jeremiah is tempted to keep silent and not to proclaim the word of the Lord (verse 8), all in an effort to avoid persecution he exclaims:

> If I say, "I will not mention him or speak anymore in his name," there is in my heart as it were a burning fire shut up in my bones, and I am weary with holding it in, and I cannot **(Jeremiah 20:9).**

The same testimony is reflected in the preaching of Isaiah. The Lord reminds him (and the future Redeemer) of his initial call (Isaiah 6) and reassures him.

> "And as for me, this is my covenant with them," says the LORD, "My Spirit that is upon you, and my words that I have put in your mouth, shall not depart out of you mouth or out of the mouth of your offspring," says the LORD, "from this time forth and forevermore" **(Isaiah 59:21).**

HOW TO SAY IT

Phinehas.	**PHI**-nee-us.
Recompence.	**REH**-kum-pence.

LESSON 10 • AUGUST 3, 2025

DAILY HOME BIBLE READINGS

MONDAY
Our Sins Testify Against Us
(Isaiah 59:1–14)

TUESDAY
Taught for Our Own Good
(Isaiah 48:12–19)

WEDNESDAY
God's Everlasting Love
(Isaiah 54:1–8)

THURSDAY
Our Redeemer is Strong
(Jeremiah 50:28–34)

FRIDAY
Walking in the Light
(Psalm 89:11–18)

SATURDAY
Redeemed with Outstretched Arm
(Exodus 6:2–8)

SUNDAY
The Lord Will Come as Redeemer
(Isaiah 59:15–21)

PREPARE FOR NEXT SUNDAY

Read **Jeremiah 7:1–15** and study "A Chance to Be Just."

Sources:

Achtemeier, Paul J., ed. *The HarperCollins Bible Dictionary*. New York: HarperCollins Publishing, 1996. 918.

Brueggemann, Walter. *Isaiah 40-66*. Louisville, KY: Westminster John Knox Press, 1998.

Goldingay, John. *Isaiah*. New International Bible Commentary. Peabody, MA: Hendrickson Publishers, 2001.

Hanson, Paul D. *Isaiah 40–66*. Interpretation. Louisville, KY: Westminster John Knox Press, 1995.

Leupold, H, C. *Exposition of Isaiah*. Grand Rapids, MI: Baker Books House, 1976.

Oswald, John N. *The Book of Isaiah, Chapters 44–66*. The New International Commentary on the Old Testament. Grand Rapids, MI: Wm. B. Eerdmans, 1998.

Simeon, Charles. *Isaiah, XXVII–LXVI*. Horae Homileticae. Vol. 8. London: Holdsworth and Ball, 1832.

Spence-Jones, H. D. M., ed. *Isaiah, Vol. II*. The Pulpit Commentary. London: Funk & Wagnalls Company, 1910.

Warren W. Wiersbe. *Be Comforted*. "Be" Commentary Series. Wheaton, IL: Victor Books, 1996.

Watts, John D. *Isaiah 34–66*. Word Biblical Commentary. Waco, TX: World Books Publishers., 1987. 286-287.

Young, Edward J. *The Book of Isaiah, Vol. 3*. Grand Rapids, MI: Wm. B. Eerdmans, 1972.

COMMENTS / NOTES:

LESSON 11 • AUGUST 10, 2025

A CHANCE TO BE JUST

BIBLE BASIS: JEREMIAH 7:1–15

BIBLE TRUTH: Through Ezra and Jeremiah, God sent messages of hope to those who will amend their ways and messages of doom to those who will not.

MEMORY VERSE: "Thus saith the LORD of hosts, the God of Israel, Amend your ways and your doing, and I will cause you to dwell in this place" (Jeremiah 7:3).

LESSON AIM: By the end of the lesson, your students will: REVIEW the messages of doom and hope found in Jeremiah; REGRET the error of their ways and resolve to change; and ADDRESS their personal unfaithfulness and their community's corruption.

BACKGROUND SCRIPTURE: Jeremiah 7:1–15; Ezra 7:6, 21–28; Jeremiah 26:8–15—Read and incorporate the insights gained from the Background Scriptures into your study of the lesson.

LESSON SCRIPTURE

ISAIAH 59:15b–21, KJV

1 The word that came to Jeremiah from the LORD, saying,

2 Stand in the gate of the LORD's house, and proclaim there this word, and say, Hear the word of the LORD, all ye of Judah, that enter in at these gates to worship the LORD.

3 Thus saith the LORD of hosts, the God of Israel, Amend your ways and your doings, and I will cause you to dwell in this place.

4 Trust ye not in lying words, saying, The temple of the LORD, The temple of the LORD, the temple of the LORD, are these.

5 For if ye thoroughly amend your ways and your doings; if ye thoroughly execute judgment between a man and his neighbour;

6 If ye oppress not the stranger, the fatherless, and the widow, and shed not innocent blood in this place, neither walk after other gods to your hurt:

7 Then will I cause you to dwell in this place, in the land that I gave to your fathers, for ever and ever.

8 Behold, ye trust in lying words, that cannot profit.

9 Will ye steal, murder, and commit adultery, and swear falsely, and burn incense unto Baal, and walk after other gods whom ye know not;

10 And come and stand before me in this house, which is called by my name, and say, We are delivered to do all these abominations?

11 Is this house, which is called by my name, become a den of robbers in your eyes? Behold, even I have seen it, saith the LORD.

12 But go ye now unto my place which was in Shiloh, where I set my name at the first, and see what I did to it for the wickedness of my people Israel.

13 And now, because ye have done all these works, saith the LORD, and I spake unto you, rising up early and speaking,

LESSON 11 • AUGUST 10, 2025

but ye heard not; and I called you, but ye answered not;

14 Therefore will I do unto this house, which is called by my name, wherein ye trust, and unto the place which I gave to you and to your fathers, as I have done to Shiloh.

15 And I will cast you out of my sight, as I have cast out all your brethren, even the whole seed of Ephraim.

BIBLICAL DEFINITIONS

Lesson 10. A. Amend (Jeremiah 7:3, 5) *yatav* (Heb.)—To reform; to make well or right.

B. Abominations (v. 10) *to'evah* (Heb.)— Idolatrous practices; various kinds of wickedness.

LIFE NEED FOR TODAY'S LESSON

AIM: Students will know people show partiality, oppress the weak, and break the law as though they are unaware of the error of their ways.

INTRODUCTION
Preach, Jeremiah, Preach!

The occasion for Jeremiah's sermon was most likely the beginning of one of the Israelite pilgrimage festivals, when great crowds of people would be pouring into the temple courts for worship. Most scholars date the chapter 7 sermon to around 609 B.C., during the first year of the reign of King Jehoiakim (**Jeremiah 26:1**). This is significant because it was some 110 years after the Northern Kingdom of Israel had fallen to the Assyrians. Jeremiah frequently points to the fall of Israel as an example of God's judgment upon a sinful and unrepentant nation, and he repeatedly warns that Judah and Jerusalem are destined for the same fate if they do not repent. The people of Judah were well aware of Israel's fate, but they had come to believe that because they had the temple, God would never judge them in the same way.

BIBLE LEARNING
AIM: Students will discover how Jeremiah speaks to the issues of oppression and abuse of strangers, orphans, and widows.

I. The Lord of the Temple (Jeremiah 7:1–3)

During the pilgrimage festivals, it would not have been unusual for pilgrims entering the temple area to be greeted by a representative of the temple asking them to examine their lives before going in for worship. On this particular day, that representative was Jeremiah. But his pleas on that day had a sense of urgency about them. Beyond the usual call for repentance, Jeremiah conveyed that their words of repentance must be accompanied by actions of abandoning their evil ways.

Jeremiah's Temple Sermon (verses 1–3)

1 The word that came to Jeremiah from the LORD, saying, 2 Stand in the gate of the LORD's house, and proclaim there this word, and say, Hear the word of the LORD, all ye of Judah, that enter in at these gates to worship the LORD. 3 Thus saith the LORD of hosts, the God of Israel, Amend your ways and your doings, and I will cause you to dwell in this place.

When Josiah became king of Israel, a priest found a copy of the Word of God in the temple, and Josiah led the nation in a religious revival that sought to restore the people's worship of God to its rightful place. However, King Josiah was slain in a battle with an Egyptian pharaoh, and when Jehoiakim replaced Josiah as king, he immediately began to reverse the religious reforms that had been instituted. Judah was caught in the middle of a battle between Egypt and Babylon over who would control Palestine, raising questions of national security and prosperity. Under Jehoiakim, worship within the temple had become ritualistic with more emphasis on the external matters of the temple than proper worship of God. The people had a form of godliness, but it was only external. They attended the temple as required, paid their tithes, and submitted their sacrificial offerings, but it was only for show. When they were not in the temple, the people committed the same evils as the heathens around them. It was under these circumstances that God instructs Jeremiah to stand in the "gate" (Heb. *sha'ar*, **SHAH-ar**) of the Lord's "house" (Heb. *bayit*, **BAH-yith**, dwelling or habitation) to proclaim a word to the entering people of Judah. The gate where Jeremiah stood was the gate that led into the court of the women and the outer court of the temple, or the court of the Gentiles. The prophet's message, then, was directed toward all those religious people within the nation that still attempted to worship God. For preaching this message, called the Temple Sermon, Jeremiah's life was threatened (see **Jeremiah 26:7–9**).

QUESTION 1
What did it mean for the people of Judah to amend their ways (**Jeremiah 7:3**)?

II. THE LONGING FOR CHANGE (verses 4–7)

Through His servant Jeremiah, God makes it very clear that continued blessings are conditional on the people's making drastic changes in their attitudes and actions. If the people stopped their evil deeds, He would allow them to continue to live in the land and have access to the temple. It was clearly the people's choice: they must choose to do justice, and treat those around and among them with respect and honor. So important was this issue of justice, and its conditional tie to living in the Promised Land, that it was included in the Ten Commandments: "Honor your father and your mother, so that you may live long in the land the LORD your God is giving you" (**Exodus 20:12, NIV**).

The Sins of the People (verses 4–7)

4 Trust ye not in lying words, saying, The temple of the LORD, The temple of the LORD, The temple of the LORD, are these. 5 For if ye throughly amend your ways and your doings; if ye throughly execute judgment between a man and his neighbor; 6 If ye oppress not the stranger, the fatherless, and the widow, and shed not innocent blood in this place, neither walk after other gods to your hurt: 7 Then will I cause you to dwell in this place, in the land that I gave to your fathers, for ever and ever.

The nation of Israel collectively embraced a misunderstanding of God's relationship with them. Because they were His chosen people and He had located His temple among them, they believed that no harm could befall them. Almost like a charm, the people would reply "the temple of the LORD" whenever they felt threatened. By doing so, they were asserting that they could do as they pleased and "trust" (Heb. *batach*, **bah-TAKH**, to feel safe or confident in) God would protect them because His home was with them. Further, the nation of Israel was under the impression that they could not be displaced from "the land" (Heb. *'erets*, **EH-rets**, land, country or territory) because God had promised it to their "forefathers" (Heb. *'ab*, **AHV**) and they believed it was their inheritance forever. What Jeremiah sought to make them understand was that God did not bestow the nation with a covenant without obligation. Only as the nation faithfully observed the requirements of their covenant with the Lord, would He honor His portion of the covenant with them. They would have to "throughly amend their ways" and "throughly execute judgment." These two phrases are examples of the Hebrew infinitive absolute. This form of verb is meant to convey intensity. In other words, the Lord wanted the people to "really amend their ways" and "truly execute judgment." Jeremiah, here, begins a representative listing of the sins Judah had committed.

III. THE LITANY OF SINS (vv. 8–11)

Here God shows that He not only knows His people's evil deeds, but He also knows their corrupt view of the temple and their worship there. The people were guilty of violating at least five of the Ten Commandments, yet they confidently flocked to the temple, where they believed their mere attendance and participation in rituals would atone for their sins. God is obviously angry both at their sins, and at their attitude that temple worship gave them indulgence to keep on sinning. He says they have turned His temple into a "den of robbers" (**Jeremiah 7:11**).

God is Watching (verses 8–11)

8 Behold, ye trust in lying words, that cannot profit. 9 Will ye steal, murder, and commit adultery, and swear falsely, and burn incense unto Baal, and walk after other gods whom ye know not; 10 And come and stand before me in this house, which is called by my name, and say, We are delivered to do all these abominations? 11 Is this house, which is called by my name, become a den of robbers in your eyes? Behold, even I have seen it, saith the LORD.

It is easy to imagine that as Jeremiah stood in the gate of the temple and continued his sermon to the nation of Israel, the people and their leadership would have become angrier with him. They had been coming to the temple to bring their offerings as they believed the Law demanded; what then was God's problem? Jeremiah was trying to show them that they had an outward show of religiosity but were inwardly corrupt. The nation of Judah assumed that their presence in the temple was all that was needed. "We are delivered" (Heb. *natsal*, **nah-TSAL**, to take away or snatch away, e.g., from violence) was the phrase used as license for them to live as they pleased when not in the temple. God would deliver them out of harm's way because His house was among them. The list of sins Jeremiah recounts for the people accuses them of violating nearly all the Ten Commandments God had handed down (**Exodus 20; Deuteronomy 5**), and though they retreated to God's house as though it were a "den" (Heb. *me'arah*, **muh-ah-RAH**, hideout) to which robbers would escape once they committed their evil deeds, it was not enough to protect them from God's wrath. God had been watching and had "seen" (Heb. *ra'ah*, **rah-AH**, to inspect, perceive, or consider) their wrong doings.

QUESTION 2
What did the people's chant say about their attitude toward God and their sin (**vv. 4, 10**)?

IV. THE LAST WARNING (vv. 12–15)

Shiloh, located about thirty miles north of Jerusalem in the Northern Kingdom of Israel, was an important place of worship during the time of the Judges (c. 1,300 B.C.–1,030 B.C.), as the tabernacle was set up there for a time. The hearers of Jeremiah's temple gate sermon were well aware that the tabernacle, an earlier forerunner to the Jerusalem temple, had been destroyed in Shiloh many hundreds of years previous. **Psalm 78:59–62** records the fate of that once sacred place of worship: "God … was filled with wrath … so that He abandoned the dwelling place at Shiloh." God would not be bound to any physical building, location, or place of worship.

Rebellious Consequences (verses 12–15)

12 But go ye now unto my place which was in Shiloh, where I set my name at the first, and see what I did to it for the wickedness of my people Israel. 13 And now, because ye have done all these works, saith the LORD, and I spake unto you, rising up early and speaking, but ye heard not; and I called you, but ye answered not; 14 Therefore will I do unto this house, which is called by my name, wherein ye trust, and unto the place which I gave to you and to your fathers, as I have done to Shiloh. 15 And I will cast you out of my sight, as I have cast out all your brethren, even the whole seed of Ephraim.

Jeremiah now seeks to reinforce for the nation of Judah the truth: trusting in a location will not preserve them from God's wrath. God challenges the people to visit Shiloh (Heb. *Shilo*, **shee-LOH**), a city in Ephraim and temporary home of the Ark of the Covenant and the Tabernacle, and view how He permitted it to be destroyed because of the wickedness of the Jewish nation at that time. The Jews at that time even brought out the Ark of the Covenant before their enemy, the Philistines, in an effort to secure their victory over them. However, the Israelites were defeated and the Ark was carried off into the land of the Philistines (**1 Samuel 4: 10**). Jeremiah was seeking to teach the people of Judah that God's favor is not tied to a location, but rather the covenant made with His people. Violation of the covenant, regardless of the location, would result in punishment.

At Shiloh, God demonstrated that He would remove His tabernacle to Jerusalem, where it now resided, and He could just as easily remove His temple from Jerusalem. God declares then that He tried to reason with the nation of Judah, "rising up early" (implying an earnestness) and speaking to them, only to have His plea for a return to righteousness fall on deaf ears. Therefore, God promises to do two things to them because of their rebellious state: 1) He will permit the enemies of Judah to conquer them, and 2) He will permit His chosen people to be carried off into captivity the same way that He permitted the seed of Ephraim (i.e, the Northern Kingdom) to be carried off.

BIBLE APPLICATION

AIM: Students will acknowledge that the state of one's heart matters to God.

Like the Israelites of Jeremiah's day, each of us daily faces temptations to perpetuate injustices and commit sinful acts. We must make choices and face their consequences. This text should also inform our attitudes and practices concerning worship and redemption. Sometimes we treat our church the way the Israelites treated their temple. We are sometimes focused on appearances and rituals rather than the God who is supposed to be the object of our worship.

STUDENTS' RESPONSES

AIM: Students will respond to the conviction of their sins by repenting.

Often our attempts at repentance and reform fall short because we simply forget what God requires of us and only talk about change in a general way. In order to combat this tendency, write down a list of resolutions and practices that will specifically help you to to "throughly amend your ways" (**Jeremiah 7:5**).

PRAYER

God, help us and guide us to follow Your ways. We do not want to worship our church instead of You. Lord, You truly deserve our praise and adoration. In Jesus' name we pray. Amen.

DIGGING DEEPER:
There is a Condition –
On the Conditional Nature of Old Testament Prophecy

The prophets' message is conditional. In other words, when people change their attitude toward God, God will change his attitude toward that people. After presenting the prophet with an acted parable, God lays out the principle in Jeremiah 18. Note the repeated us of the word "if" that points to the conditional nature of the prophecies.

If at any time I declare concerning a nation of a kingdom, that I will pluck up and break down and destroy it, if that nation concerning which I have spoken turns from its evil, [then] I will relent of the disaster that I intended to do to it. And if at any time I declare concerning a nation or a kingdom that I will build and plant it, and if it does evil in my sight, not listening to my voice, then I will relent of the good that I had intended to do to it (Jeremiah 7-10).

A prime example of the conditional nature of prophecies is Jonah. He is given the command to go to Ninevah (1:2; 3:2) and announce the coming judgment of God in forty days (3:4). Then the Bible tells us that the people of Ninevah believed God and they demonstrated their repentance by fasting and putting on sackcloth (3:5). Here is the evidence of the conditional nature of the prophecy:

When God saw what they did, how they turned from their evil way, God relented of the disaster that he has said he would do to them, and he did not do it (Jonah 3:10).

The word of the prophet was not the final word. If the people repented, God would change his mind.

HOW TO SAY IT

Throughly.   thru-LEE.
Shiloh.   SHY-lo.

DAILY HOME BIBLE READINGS

MONDAY
Justice for the Poor
(Psalm 140:6–13)

TUESDAY
My People Have Forgotten Me
(Jeremiah 18:11–17)

WEDNESDAY
Judgment for the Disobedient
(Ezra 7:21–28)

THURSDAY
If You Will Not Listen
(Jeremiah 26:1–7)

FRIDAY
Amend Your Ways and Your Doings
(Jeremiah 26:8–15)

SATURDAY
God Abandoned Shiloh
(Psalm 78:56–62)

SUNDAY
Let Me Dwell with You
(Jeremiah 7:1–15)

PREPARE FOR NEXT SUNDAY

Read **Ezekiel 18:1–13, 31–32** and study "A Call for Repentance."

Sources:
Brown, Francis. *The Brown-Driver-Briggs Hebrew and English Lexicon*. Peabody, MA: Hendrickson, 2010.
Burton, James. *Coffman Commentaries on the Old Testament and New Testament*. Abilene, TX: Abilene Christian University Press, n.d.
Craigie, Peter, Page Kelley, and Joel Drinkard Jr. *Jeremiah 1–25*. Word Biblical Commentary. Vol. 6. Nashville, TN: Thomas Nelson, 1991.
Dunn, James D. G. and John W. Rogerson. *Commentary on the Bible*. Grand Rapids, MI: Wm. B. Eerdmans, 2003.
English, E. Schuyler and Marian Bishop Bower, eds. *The Holy Bible: Pilgrim Edition*. New York: Oxford University Press, Inc., 1952.

LESSON 11 • AUGUST 10, 2025

Espinosa, Eddie. *Songs of Faith and Praise*. Alton H. Howard, editor. West Monroe, LA: Howard Publishing, 1994.

Feinberg, Charles. Jeremiah. *The Expositor's Bible Commentary*. Vol. 6. Frank Gaebelein, editor. Grand Rapids: Zondervan, 1986.

Howley, G. C. D., F. F. Bruce, and H. L. Ellison. *The New Layman's Bible Commentary*. Grand Rapids, MI: Zondervan Publishing, 1979.

Life Application Study Bible. New Living Translation. Carol Stream, IL: Tyndale House Publishers, 2007.

Strong, James. *Strong's Exhaustive Concordance of the Bible*. Nashville, TN: Thomas Nelson, 1990.

Wolf, Herbert. Judges. *The Expositor's Bible Commentary*. Vol. 3. Frank Gaebelein, editor. Grand Rapids, MI: Zondervan, 1992.

COMMENTS / NOTES:

LESSON 12 • AUGUST 17, 2025

A CALL FOR REPENTANCE

BIBLE BASIS: EZEKIEL 18:1-13, 31-32

BIBLE TRUTH: Ezekiel advises confession and, along with Proverbs, exhorts the people to do the right thing and thereby build a just community.

MEMORY VERSE: "Repent, and turn from your sins! Don't let them destroy you! Put all your rebellion behin you, and find yourselves a new heart and a new spirit" (from Ezekiel 18:30-31).

LESSON AIM: By the end of the lesson, your students will: REVIEW the message of Ezekiel that God holds each person responsible for his or her own actions; FEEL accountability for personal acts of omission that damage the community; and PRAY for discernment in how to amend our ways and build communities of justice.

BACKGROUND SCRIPTURE: Ezekiel 18; Proverbs 21:2-15; Hosea 14—Read and incorporate the insights gained from the Background Scriptures into your study of the lesson.

LESSON SCRIPTURE

EZEKIEL 18:1-13, 31-32, KJV

1 The word of the LORD came unto me again, saying,

2 What mean ye, that ye use this proverb concerning the land of Israel, saying, The fathers have eaten sour grapes, and the children's teeth are set on edge?

3 As I live, saith the Lord GOD, ye shall not have occasion any more to use this proverb in Israel.

4 Behold, all souls are mine; as the soul of the father, so also the soul of the son is mine: the soul that sinneth, it shall die.

5 But if a man be just, and do that which is lawful and right,

6 And hath not eaten upon the mountains, neither hath lifted up his eyes to the idols of the house of Israel, neither hath defiled his neighbour's wife, neither hath come near to a menstruous woman,

7 And hath not oppressed any, but hath restored to the debtor his pledge, hath spoiled none by violence, hath given his bread to the hungry, and hath covered the naked with a garment;

8 He that hath not given forth upon usury, neither hath taken any increase, that hath withdrawn his hand from iniquity, hath executed true judgment between man and man,

9 Hath walked in my statutes, and hath kept my judgments, to deal truly; he is just, he shall surely live, saith the Lord GOD.

10 If he beget a son that is a robber, a shedder of blood, and that doeth the like to any one of these things,

11 And that doeth not any of those duties, but even hath eaten upon the mountains, and defiled his neighbour's wife,

12 Hath oppressed the poor and needy, hath spoiled by violence, hath not restored the pledge, and hath lifted up his eyes to the idols, hath committed abomination,

LESSON 12 • AUGUST 17, 2025

13 Hath given forth upon usury, and hath taken increase: shall he then live ? he shall not live: he hath done all these abominations; he shall surely die; his blood shall be upon him.

31 Cast away from you all your transgressions, whereby ye have transgressed; and take you a new heart and a new spirit: for why will ye die, O house of Israel?

32 For I have no pleasure in the death of him that dieth, saith the Lord GOD: wherefore turn yourselves, and live ye.

BIBLICAL DEFINITIONS

A. Soul (Ezekiel 18:4) *nefesh* (Heb.)—Life, creature, the inner being of a person.

B. Cast away (v. 31) *shalak* (Heb.)—To throw away, cast off, shed, cast down.

LIFE NEED FOR TODAY'S LESSON

AIM: Students will become aware of behavior that is harmful to the life of a community.

INTRODUCTION
The Blame Game

Ezekiel's sermon in this lesson was preached to an audience of Israelites living in exile in Babylonia. They were foreigners living in a strange land, having a very hard time making sense of all the bad things that had happened to them.

They had placed their hope in the temple and the God of their forefathers. They felt both helpless and hopeless. They blamed their current fate on the failures and sins of the generations before them. They no doubt just felt like giving up on their past, including their faith and their God, and were just trying to make the best of a bad situation.

God had called Ezekiel to minister to these people of little hope. God had told him that this would not be an easy assignment. He had said these people were "rebellious ... obstinate and stubborn" and not likely to listen (**Ezekiel 2:3–5**). Ezekiel would need to employ some creative ways of communicating to the Israelites, including using dramatic object lessons, and speaking in parables, as he does here. Through it all, Ezekiel was fearlessly faithful as God's prophet. We can only hope that some of his original audience heeded his warnings, and that we heed them ourselves today.

BIBLE LEARNING
AIM: Students will learn that God's rewards those who seek to build healthy communities and to please God.

I. The Proverb from the Past (Ezekiel 18:1–4)

The people of Judah, exiles in a foreign land, rationalized that they were being punished for the sinful deeds of their ancestors. There was a popular, though not scriptural, proverb in those days that reflected this sentiment: "The fathers have eaten sour grapes, and the children's teeth are set on edge." Apparently God was tired of hearing this proverb tossed about as a fatalistic and irresponsible view of the consequences of sin (**vv. 2–3**). He says He has heard it enough and He doesn't want to hear it any more, so He bans its use.

Father and Son (verses 1–4)

1 The word of the LORD came unto me again, saying, **2** What mean ye, that ye use this proverb concerning the land of Israel, saying, The fathers have eaten sour grapes, and the children's teeth are set on edge?

LESSON 12 • AUGUST 17, 2025

When things do not go as well as one might want, the natural tendency is to complain and try to put the blame on another. This had occurred so often within the land of Israel that it had developed into a "proverb" (Heb. *mashal*, **mah-SHAHL**, a proverbial saying or aphorism) (see **Jeremiah 31:29–30**). Because of the sins of the "fathers" (Heb. *'ab*, **AHV**, the father, head, or founder of a household, group, or clan), the children were being made to pay the penalty. Some support for the belief that the children were being made to pay the penalty for the sins of their fathers can be found in **Exodus 20:5**; **34:7** (cf. **Joshua 7:19–25**; **2 Kings 24:1–4**). The nation of Israel was conquered and driven into exile because of the apostasy of Manasseh.

Only by this means could the sin be removed. However, within the nation of Israel, the teaching had been carried to excess and was being used to remove personal responsibility for sins.

3 As I live, saith the Lord GOD, ye shall not have occasion any more to use this proverb in Israel. 4 Behold, all souls are mine; as the soul of the father, so also the soul of the son is mine: the soul that sinneth, it shall die.

God as the Creator and Father of all affirms that all "souls" are His (Heb. *nephesh*, **NEH-fesh**, a living being with life in the blood) and that He has the right to impose penalty for wrongdoing. God knew that there was a natural tendency in people for the son to follow the sins of the father and thereby share the father's guilt. For that reason, there was no room for the children to complain that they were being punished unfairly. The prophet Jeremiah offered that the sins of the father would be visited on the children (see **32:18**). If the father lived in rebellion to God and His precepts, then there was every possibility that the son would follow in the same rebellion. Beginning with this verse, Ezekiel begins to offer a corrective to the misunderstanding of God's intent, which had grown into a common proverb by stating that "the soul that sinneth" would be the soul that "died" (Heb. *mut*, **MOOTH**, to perish). In other words, the individual person was responsible for his or her own sin and its consequences.

QUESTION 1
What does God say about the soul of the father and the son (**Ezekiel 18:4**)?

II. THE PARABLE; PROMISE OF LIFE FOR A RIGHTEOUS MAN (vv. 5–9)

Ezekiel uses a parable to illustrate his point about individual responsibility and punishment for sins.

Living a Just Life (verses 5–9)

5 But if a man be just, and do that which is lawful and right,

The laws determining what was "lawful" (Heb. *mishpat*, **mish-PAHT**, justice or fairness) and "right" (Heb. *tsedaqah*, **tsehdah-KAH**, honesty, loyalty, or justness) were spelled out in Mosaic Torah, including Exodus, Deuteronomy, and the Holiness Code in **Leviticus 17–26**. Many of these laws were more detailed expressions of the Ten Commandments (**Exodus 20:1–17**) and the greatest commandments of loving God and loving neighbor (**Deuteronomy 6:5, Leviticus 19:18**). In this way, a man was to be righteous in the eyes of God but also dealt justly with those around him.

6 And hath not eaten upon the mountains, neither hath lifted up his eyes to the idols of the house of Israel, neither hath defiled his neighbor's wife, neither hath come near to a menstruous woman, 7 And hath not oppressed any, but hath restored to the debtor his pledge, hath spoiled none by violence, hath

given his bread to the hungry, and hath covered the naked with a garment; 8 He that hath not given forth upon usury, neither hath taken any increase, that hath withdrawn his hand from iniquity, hath executed true judgment between man and man, 9 Hath walked in my statutes, and hath kept my judgments, to deal truly; he is just, he shall surely live, saith the Lord GOD.

The righteous man was one who did not participate in ritual meals on mountain-top sanctuaries, which was the practice of the pagans (cf. **6:2-4; 20:28-29**), nor indulged in the worship of idols (cf. **Leviticus 19:4**), did not commit adultery (cf. **Exodus 20:14**), did not approach a menstruating woman (cf. **Leviticus 18:19**), did not violate the laws governing business practices (cf. **Exodus 22:25**), fed the hungry, clothed the naked, and judged fairly (cf. **Leviticus 19:15**). God declares that this individual shall live.

III. THE PARABLE CONTINUED; PUNISHMENT FOR AN UNRIGHTEOUS SON (vv. 10-13)

Ezekiel continues his parable by presenting the imaginary son who is the antithesis of all his father's good characteristics. He is not faithful to God, and he treats his neighbors with contempt. He is a thief and a liar, oppresses the poor, and withholds justice. Ezekiel says God will judge this man for his sins, and he deserves death. His father's righteousness could not save him from bearing responsibility and punishment for his own actions.

Bad Choices Lead to Bad Consequences (verses 10-13)

10 If he beget a son that is a robber, a shedder of blood, and that doeth the like to any one of these things, 11 And that doeth not any of those duties, but even hath eaten upon the mountains, and defiled his neighbor's wife, 12 Hath oppressed the poor and needy, hath spoiled by violence, hath not restored the pledge, and hath lifted up his eyes to the idols, hath committed abomination, 13 Hath given forth upon usury, and hath taken increase: shall he then live? he shall not live: he hath done all these abominations; he shall surely die; his blood shall be upon him.

However, if the same individual has a son who is guilty of being a thief, a killer, of any of those things expressly forbidden in the Torah, then this son "shall surely die," reinforcing the principle that the consequence of his actions will only be upon him.

IV. THE PLEADING FOR REPENTANCE (vv. 31-32)

The destruction of Israel, Jerusalem, and the temple was God's judgment and punishment for the spiritual apostasy and moral decay of the previous generations. But He speaks through Ezekiel to tell the exiled Israelites that their situation is as much a judgment of their sins as a national punishment for their fathers' sins. God justly judges each person individually. One person's sins may affect other lives, even the entire community. But God does not punish anyone for another's sins. Each person is responsible for his own actions.

New Way of Being (verses 31-32)

31 Cast away from you all your transgressions, whereby ye have transgressed; and make you a new heart and a new spirit: for why will ye die, O house of Israel?

Ezekiel pleads on God's behalf for the nation of Israel to turn away from all its "transgressions." They are to do their part to "make a new heart" (Heb. *leb*, **LEV**, heart, mind, or inclination) and also to make a "new spirit" (Heb. *ruach*, **ROO-akh**, spirit, breath, mental and spiritual essence of the human or divine). The prophet wants the people to understand that the cause of their sin resides within themselves and that the only sure way to escape sin's consequences is to be reconciled to God (see **Romans 7:21–8:2**). Ezekiel implores the people to acquire a new heart, a task that is impossible for us to do, but trying to do so teaches us what God desires of us and brings with it the realization that God alone can make our hearts new. So too with the spirit: man does not have the ability to make a new spirit for himself, but the effort drives man to see his own helplessness and seek God's Holy Spirit to accomplish the task. Ezekiel is telling the people that they need not die, because God will honor their sincere repentance with an abundance of His grace.

32 For I have no pleasure in the death of him that dieth, saith the Lord GOD: wherefore turn yourselves, and live ye.

Ezekiel concludes this entreaty by reminding the nation of Israel that God takes no "pleasure" (Heb. *chapats*, **khah-FAHTS**, to delight or take joy in) in the death of the wicked. All that is required is to sincerely turn from wickedness, repent, and experience God's grace. God is merciful and desires that all find life in Him and "live" (Heb. *chayah*, **khah-YAH**, to restore to life or quicken) (see **2 Peter 3:9**).

QUESTION 2
What does Ezekiel show as the appropriate response when we are tempted to blame others for our situation (**v. 31**)?

BIBLE APPLICATION
AIM: Students will understand that they are responsible for their actions.

Perhaps you or someone you know feels like they are suffering because of the actions of others. Perhaps your parents were substance abusers, or were absent during your formative years. Perhaps you were abused physically or emotionally. Perhaps you just don't feel loved and appreciated, and have given up hope for a better future. When people are without hope, it is easy to blame someone else, and turn to gangs, drugs, or alcohol as an escape. Your situation may indeed be miserable. But God's Word assures us that we are not bound to our present condition. There is hope, life, and joy to be found in the loving community of faith that is the family of God.

STUDENTS' RESPONSES
AIM: Students will respond to conviction of their sins by repenting.

Sometimes taking responsibility for our own actions, acknowledging our sin, and turning from it is very difficult to do. If you are struggling with this, seek the guidance of a spiritually mature trusted friend. Jesus has already won the victory over our sin and the penalty of death. What joy there is in allowing Him to transform your thinking from that of victim to victor! He will give you a new heart and a new spirit, one in which you will find joy in helping others, and in building and maintaining healthy relationships in a healthy community.

PRAYER
Lord, create in us a renewed spirit and a willing heart to care for others and ourselves in ways that are pleasing and just before You. You are gracious and kind to give us the opportunity to witness to others about our faith in Christ. In Jesus' name we pray. Amen.

Digging Deeper:
I'm Just a Messenger
A recurring refrain in the writings of the prophets is, "The word of the LORD came to …" This is a formula that identifies the words spoken by God's prophet to his people. By definition, a prophet is a spokesperson for

God, who declares God's message (i.e., prophecy) to God's people. As widely noted, priests were the people's representative to God, while prophets were God's representative to people. This is reflected in the terms used for prophets. For example, the designation "Man of God" speaks of the moral character of the prophet. True prophets are people of integrity. The greatest prophet of the Old Testament was Moses (Deuteronomy 33:1). Likewise, Saul called Samuel a "man of God," whose prophecies come to pass (1 Samuel 9:6). In that same context, the Bible writer of 1 Samuel informs us that prophets were also called "seers" (1 Samuel 9:9). Another label is one that God uses to describe the prophets: "my servant" (Joshua 1:1-2; Jeremiah 7:25).

Finally, the prophet was called a "messenger of the LORD." The idea behind this title is that the prophet has a divine message to communicate. He has been in the presence of God, received a message from God, and must now convey that message to God's people (cf. Jeremiah 15:19). Whatever the prophet says has the authority of heaven behind it. People can choose to respond or ignore the message with attending blessings or consequences. Nevertheless, they cannot ignore that they received a message: "Thus says the LORD."

HOW TO SAY IT
Usury. USE-uh-ree.

Executed. EK-se-kyu-tid.

DAILY HOME BIBLE READINGS

MONDAY
Justice, Righteousness, and Repentance (Isaiah 1:24–28)

TUESDAY
Justice: A Joy to the Righteous (Proverbs 21:10–15)

WEDNESDAY
Avoiding a Parent's Negative Example (Ezekiel 18:14–19)

THURSDAY
The Consequences of Changing Behaviors (Ezekiel 18:21–28)

FRIDAY
The Lord Weighs the Heart (Proverbs 21:2–8)

SATURDAY
Walking in the Lord's Ways (Hosea 14)

SUNDAY
The Person Who Sins Shall Die (Ezekiel 18:1–13, 31–32)

PREPARE FOR NEXT SUNDAY
Read **Zechariah 7:8–14** and study "God Demands Justice."

Sources:
Brown, Francis. *The Brown-Driver-Briggs Hebrew and English Lexicon.* Peabody MA: Hendrickson, 2010.
Burton, James. *Coffman Commentaries on the Old Testament and New Testament.* Abilene, TX: Abilene Christian University Press, n.d.
Duguid, Iain M. Ezekiel. *The NIV Application Commentary.* Grand Rapids, MI: Zondervan, 1999.
Dunn, James D. G. and John W. Rogerson. *Commentary on the Bible.* Grand Rapids, MI: Wm. B. Eerdmans, 2003.
English, E. Schuyler and Marian Bishop Bower, eds. *The Holy Bible: Pilgrim Edition.* New York: Oxford University Press, 1952.
Howley, G.C.D., F.F. Bruce, and H.L. Ellison. *The New Layman's Bible Commentary.* Grand Rapids, MI: Zondervan, 1979.
Life Application Study Bible. New Living Translation. Carol Stream, IL: Tyndale House Publishers, 2007.
Rainer, Thom S. *Baptist Hymnal.* Nashville, TN: LifeWay, 2008.
Strong, James. *Strong's Exhaustive Concordance of the Bible.* Nashville, TN: Thomas Nelson, 1990.

LESSON 13 • AUGUST 24, 2025

GOD DEMANDS JUSTICE

BIBLE BASIS: ZECHARIAH 7:8–14

BIBLE TRUTH: God requires kindness and mercy for the widows, orphans, aliens, and the poor. The Lord will also heal the wounds of the afflicted and shower prosperity on the people.

MEMORY VERSE: "Thus speaketh the LORD of hosts, saying, Execute true judgment, and shew mercy and compassions every man to his brother: and oppress not the widow, nor the fatherless, the stranger, nor the poor; and let none of you imagine evil against his brother in your heart" (Zechariah 7:9–10).

LESSON AIM: By the end of the lesson, your students will: STUDY the punishment meted out by God for those who reject His demands; MAKE CONFESSIONS concerning how we abandon the weak; and SHOW KINDNESS to the oppressed and the weak.

BACKGROUND SCRIPTURE: Zechariah 7:8–14; Isaiah 30:18–26; Psalm 147:1–11—Read and incorporate the insights gained from the Background Scriptures into your study of the lesson.

LESSON SCRIPTURE

ZECHARIAH 7:8–14, KJV

8 And the word of the LORD came unto Zechariah, saying,

9 Thus speaketh the LORD of hosts, saying, Execute true judgment, and shew mercy and compassions every man to his brother:

10 And oppress not the widow, nor the fatherless, the stranger, nor the poor; and let none of you imagine evil against his brother in your heart.

11 But they refused to hearken, and pulled away the shoulder, and stopped their ears, that they should not hear.

12 Yea, they made their hearts as an adamant stone, lest they should hear the law, and the words which the LORD of hosts hath sent in his spirit by the former prophets: therefore came a great wrath from the LORD of hosts.

13 Therefore it is come to pass, that as he cried, and they would not hear; so they cried, and I would not hear, saith the LORD of hosts:

14 But I scattered them with a whirlwind among all the nations whom they knew not. Thus the land was desolate after them, that no man passed through nor returned: for they laid the pleasant land desolate.

BIBLICAL DEFINITIONS

A. Wrath (Zechariah 7:12) *ketsef* (Heb.)—Great anger or fierce rage.

B. Desolate (v. 14) *shamem* (Heb.)—Laid waste, uninhabited, or deserted.

LIFE NEED FOR TODAY'S LESSON

AIM: Students will know that some people show no kindness, mercy, or justice to others.

LESSON 13 • AUGUST 24, 2025

INTRODUCTION
Zechariah's Prophetic Oracles

Zechariah prophesied during a time of great upheaval in the Persian Empire. Cambyses, the son of Cyrus the Great, succeeded his father, who died in 530 B.C. Then Darius took the throne after Cambyses' sudden death in 522 B.C. to inherit the job of extinguishing several rebellions that sprang up throughout the empire. At the same time, the Jews who had returned to their homeland were rebuilding the temple in Jerusalem. Zechariah was a contemporary of Haggai and they both preached to encourage the people to continue the work of rebuilding this second temple.

It is in this context that a delegation is sent to Zechariah from Bethel, the former site of idolatrous worship in the Northern Kingdom. The delegation is sent to ask whether they should continue fasting now since their seventy-year exile would soon be completed (7:3). Zechariah begins a series of prophetic oracles concerning the time of the Messiah and the renewed righteousness of the people of God.

BIBLE LEARNING
AIM: Students will learn that God consistently communicates that obedience and justice are more important than any ritualistic act.

I. The Calling (Zechariah 7:8–10)

This passage begins with God's calling for the Israelites. It is a formula that is often used in reference to their basic duties as God's covenant people. They were to "execute true judgment and shew mercy and compassions every man to his brother." These two admonitions are prominent in Scripture, especially in the prophetic writings (**Micah 6:6-8; Hosea 12:6-7**). Zechariah's prophecy gets at the heart of true covenant loyalty to God, which is not found in blindly following religious rituals such as fasting at a certain time of year, but in dealing justly with others and showing them the kindness and compassion of God.

False Worship (verses 8–10)

8 And the word of the LORD came unto Zechariah, saying,

The people of Bethel (an important and symbolic town; its name means "house of God") had sought out the priest and prophets to see if they should fast during a certain month, as was their custom. Jehovah takes this opportunity to recall to the people's minds the former prophets and their message. Zechariah realizes that Bethel's religious practice is similar to that of Israel and Judah before the exile, who were practicing religious rituals but did not have any true heart involvement or genuine repentance behind it. In light of this suspicion, he reminds the people that the prophets had, for years, warned the people about practicing ritual without true worship.

9 Thus speaketh the LORD of hosts, saying, Execute true judgment, and shew mercy and compassions every man to his brother:

At this point in the book of Zechariah, the building of the temple is well underway, so that in one sense, God's people are showing responsiveness and obedience to His command. However, it is clear from God's word through Zechariah that true covenant faithfulness is absent, as evidenced by the failure of the people to demonstrate justice and kindness in community. God's voice thunders with a verb-noun combination: *shapat* (Heb. **shah-FAHT**) and *mishpat* (Heb. **mish-PAHT**). These words are from the same Hebrew tri-consonantal root, sh-p-t, and are linked together in a phrase that might be literally translated as "judge a judgment." This word combination has a variety of meanings that, taken together, speak not only of "judgment" but of "judgment according to truth." Although the people have apparently shown some discernment and wisdom, the forceful repetition of this word group indicates that they have not extended true justice and mercy to their neighbor, even though the Lord has shown remarkable mercy to them. As a result, Jehovah demands conduct that simply reflects the way He has treated His people. "Mercy" and "compassions" do not refer to some heroic act or unreasonable demand, but the natural and proper outgrowth of the mercy the people had received from the Lord's hand.

10 And oppress not the widow, nor the fatherless, the stranger, nor the poor; and let none of you imagine evil against his brother in your heart.

Zechariah's call for justice rather than oppression repeats the calls of the prophets before the exile, as well as God's command to show mercy to the helpless (**Deuteronomy 14:29; 16:11; 24:19–21**). Although the verb *'ashaq* (Heb. **ah-SHAHK**) can often mean "defraud," "oppress" is a better translation here because, in this context, the word emphasizes the position of power in which the Israelites find themselves, relative to the helpless among them. Once again, these commands are full of sad irony: Although the Jews found themselves utterly helpless in Babylon and Persia, God showed them mercy and made a way for them to return to Jerusalem and build the temple. Yet, shockingly, the Jews have turned and looked on the powerless in their community with contempt, perhaps even taking advantage of their lowly position.

God's covenant people are supposed to mirror the covenant faithfulness He has shown them. In light of the Gospel revealed through Christ, the perfect Covenant Keeper, we understand that our failings are covered in the blood of the new covenant, shed by the Lamb. Because of Christ's sacrifice, we should strive to demonstrate His faithfulness to us in our dealings with each other!

QUESTION 1
Whom did God command them to show mercy, kindness, and tender compassion toward (**Zechariah 7:9**)?

II. THE REJECTION (vv. 11–12)
Zechariah recalls the people's past disobedience. First he goes over their initial actions in response to the words of God concerning their covenant duties of justice and compassion. The people were stubborn and would not listen to the Word of God concerning their behavior.

A Stubborn People (verses 11–12)
11 But they refused to hearken, and pulled away the shoulder, and stopped their ears, that they should not hear.

The word "hearken" in the King James Version, although not commonly used today, brings out the sense of the Hebrew word *qashab* (**kahSHAV**), which means more than just listening. It does not merely indicate that the Israelites had failed to hear the prophets' warnings; it means that they had heard these warnings all too well, but had stubbornly refused to repent and obey. Nevertheless, the focus on hearing is obvious; the phrase "pulled away the shoulder" might be expressed in more modern terms as "turned their backs" (implying a breaking of relationship and disobedience, but also making it harder to hear). The phrase translated "they stopped their ears" literally means "they made their ears heavy," suggesting that the act of listening was burdensome to them. The final clause shows the purpose of these actions on their part: They did not want to hear the warnings of the prophets, and although they no doubt heard the warnings, they made every effort to pretend that they hadn't. Zechariah's warning gains added force in that his hearers could hardly claim not to have heard him! The actions of their ancestors and the resulting destruction and despair would have made God's warning utterly impossible to ignore.

12 Yea, they made their hearts as an adamant stone, lest they should hear the law, and the words which the LORD of hosts hath sent in his spirit by the former prophets: therefore came a great wrath from the LORD of hosts.

The description of the covenant people's faithlessness continues, with a natural transition from the ears to the heart (which in the Bible always represents the center of both understanding and affections). There is no doubt who the guilty party is in this covenant violation. God did not harden their hearts, as He did with Pharaoh (**Exodus 9:12, 10:1, 20**); they hardened their own hearts. On the contrary, the prophets before the Exile portray a God longing for His people to return to Him, pining for His adulterous bride. The intentional hardening described here was heartbreaking, coming from a people who had seen the disastrous consequences of disobedience. The word used for "adamant stone" *shamir* (**shah-MEER**) is the word used for the hard point of a stylus, usually made of a kind of quartz. The people had made their hearts as hard as flint.

Zechariah mentions the Spirit as the agent of the former prophets' inspiration. This reference brings out the seriousness of not heeding their commands and warnings—to do so was to deny the very Spirit of God. The New Testament shows us that denying the Spirit is blasphemy (**Mark 3:22–30**). Ananias and Sapphira paid with their lives for what is called "lying to the Holy Spirit" (see **Acts 5:1–10**). It is no wonder that the military phrase "LORD of hosts" reappears, with God pictured as going to war against His own people! Their treason has brought about the King's inevitable response, despite centuries of patience.

QUESTION 2
What did the people do with the word that they heard through the prophet (**v. 11**)?

III. SCATTERING (vv. 13–14)
Zechariah concludes this oracle with a description of God's wrath on the nation of Judah as they refused to hear His Word. Judah's deafness to God's Word receives a reciprocal response from God to their prayers. Since they will not listen to His Word, He will not listen to their prayers. This is similar to the words of **Proverbs 28:9**: "He that turneth away his ear from hearing the law, even his prayer shall be abomination" (KJV). This is a clear example of what happens when we refuse to obey God's Word: He will refuse our prayers.

Hearing, but Not Listening (verses 13–14)

13 Therefore it is come to pass, that as he cried, and they would not hear; so they cried, and I would not hear, saith the LORD of hosts:

The verbs in this passage suggest repeated, customary actions; the Lord's call to His people was, of course, repeated many times over, as was their unbelieving response. God in His mercy patiently offered restoration far beyond what His people deserved. Eventually, however, He executed His justice in a perfectly proportional way. Because He had called to them and they had not listened, he would not hear their cries. Yet, God provided safety and security (albeit in Babylonia) for those who truly repented.

Many of these same people returned to Jerusalem and were addressed by Zechariah. For them, the importance of hearing the Lord's call was abundantly clear.

14 But I scattered them with a whirlwind among all the nations whom they knew not. Thus the land was desolate after them, that no man passed through nor returned: for they laid the pleasant land desolate.

The term translated "scattered . . . with a whirlwind" occurs seven times in the Old Testament (cf. **Isaiah 54:11; Habakkuk 3:14**), and in all but two cases, it refers to a violent storm. This is not a literal storm, however, but the worst kind of curse imaginable: exile from the Promised Land, where the people had rest, and forcible removal into the terrible strangeness of foreign lands, with strange customs and foreign gods. It is no accident that the curses of **Deuteronomy 28** focus primarily on assault and capture by a foreign people; this was the worst kind of judgment imaginable for a people whose very lifeblood, blessedness, and shalom depended on the land that had been promised to their great forefather Abraham hundreds of years earlier. And so the worst kind of upheaval took place: Whereas back in the glory days of Israel—the reigns of David and Solomon—the whole world traveled through the blessed land, now it had become desolate, without the hum of merchants traveling through it. Given that this land at the eastern end of the Mediterranean was a key crossroads, its desolation would have been a terribly striking reminder of God's rejection of His people.

As Zechariah now stands among the people to whom God has shown great mercy and restored their land, his warnings and promises focus on making sure that the people retain the blessedness promised to them. Such warnings and promises are wonderfully relevant to people who are richly blessed in Christ. Believers must both hear and obey God's commands.

QUESTION 3
What did God say He would do when the people cried (**v. 13**)?

BIBLE APPLICATION
AIM: Students will expect divine displeasure when they reject divine commands.

There are numerous problems in our society. Gangs and drugs plague our urban areas. Our national economy is unstable. Wars with other nations are a constant threat. We pray and cry out to God and observe all the outward rituals of religion, but we do not have a high priority on justice and compassion for our neighbor. If these two things had priority in our lives, then we would be able to eradicate these problems. Instead we cry out to God without listening to His Word. It is important for us not only to cry out to God, but also do what He says. Sometimes the solution to our problems lies within our own hearts as we turn back to Him.

STUDENTS' RESPONSES
AIM: Students will utilize the resources with which God has blessed them to help others.

Often justice issues are separate from our prayer life. It is possible that we have cried out to God, but He does not hear because we have not obeyed His call to show justice and compassion to those less fortunate. As an experiment, before your private times of prayer, list out ways that you can personally show justice and compassion to those around you. Once you make this list, pray for the people you will serve. Make note in the days to come whether God answers your other requests as well. Sometimes He isn't hearing us because we aren't hearing Him.

LESSON 13 • AUGUST 24, 2025

PRAYER

God of justice and compassion, Your love for those who need Your guidance is a very present reality. Give us the resources, the hope, and the fortitude to help others. Your love never fails, so let us in love, be the light of hope to others. In Jesus' name we pray. Amen.

Digging Deeper
Should We Fast?

What religious practices is the prophet Zechariah referring to in chapter 7? The date of the prophecy is given in verse 1: the fourth year of King Darius … on the fourth day of the ninth month, which is Chislev (i.e., December 4, 518 B.C.). The text says that the people of Bethel sent a delegation to the priests and priest of the house of the Lord and the prophets (verse 2). Here was the question: Should we continue to practice the four annual fasts as we have for the past 70 years during the exile in Babylon? These fast observed the events that surrounded the downfall of Jerusalem in 586 B.C.:

1. The taking of Jerusalem by Nebuchadnezzar in the fourth month (Jeremiah 52:6).
2. The burning of the temple in the fifth month (Jeremiah 52:12)
3. The murder of Gedaliah the governor in the seventh month (Jeremiah 41:1-2)
4. The siege of Jerusalem in the tenth month (2 Kings 25:1)

Given that the reconstruction of the temple in Jerusalem is proceeding so well, should we continue to "weep and abstain in the fifth month" (verse 3), a practice that commemorated the burning of the original temple? God's response is given through the prophet in chapters 7 and 8 (note the repeated use of the phrase, "Thus says the Lord of hosts"). In essence, His answer is, "No, you are not required to keep those fasts. They were never ordered by Me. Rather, you should keep the commands given by the former prophets (Zechariah 7:7), namely, to love God and keep the Mosaic laws (Zechariah 7:9-10).

HOW TO SAY IT

Hearken.	**HAR**-ken.
Adamant.	**AH**-duh-ment.

DAILY HOME BIBLE READINGS

MONDAY
You Behaved Worse than Your Ancestors (Jeremiah 16:9–13)

TUESDAY
I Call Upon the Lord (2 Samuel 22:1–7)

WEDNESDAY
Hope in God's Steadfast Love (Psalm 147:1–11)

THURSDAY
Walking in the Way (Judges 2:16–23)

FRIDAY
Pursue Justice and Only Justice (Deuteronomy 16:16–20)

SATURDAY
The Lord Waits to Be Gracious (Isaiah 30:18–26)

SUNDAY
The Results of Not Listening (Zechariah 7:8–14)

PREPARE FOR NEXT SUNDAY

Read **Malachi 3:1–10** and study "Return to a Just God."

Sources:
Burton, James. *Coffman Commentaries on the Old Testament and New Testament.* Abilene, TX: Abilene Christian University Press, n.d.
Dunn, James D. G. and John W. Rogerson. *Commentary on the Bible.* Grand Rapids, MI: Wm. B. Eerdmans, 2003.
Howley, G.C.D., F.F. Bruce, and H.L. Ellison. *The New Layman's Bible Commentary.* Grand Rapids, MI: Zondervan, 1979.

LESSON 14 • AUGUST 31, 2025

RETURN TO A JUST GOD

BIBLE BASIS: MALACHI 3:1–10

BIBLE TRUTH: God requires justice and faithfulness and will bestow bountiful blessings in many ways.

MEMORY VERSE: "Even from the days of your fathers ye are gone away from mine ordinances, and have not kept them. Return unto me, and I will return unto you, saith the LORD of hosts. But ye said, Wherein shall we return?" (Malachi 3:7).

LESSON AIM: By the end of this lesson, your students will: REVIEW Malachi's prophecy about possessions, wealth, and hospitality in light of our faithfulness and justice; CONFESS personal unfaithfulness to God and PRAY for forgiveness; and institute a personal plan for charitable living.

BACKGROUND SCRIPTURE: Malachi 3:1–10; Matthew 7:12; Psalm 24:4–11— Read and incorporate the insights gained from the Background Scriptures into your study of the lesson.

LESSON SCRIPTURE

MALACHI 3:1–10, KJV

1 Behold, I will send my messenger, and he shall prepare the way before me: and the LORD, whom ye seek, shall suddenly come to his temple, even the messenger of the covenant, whom ye delight in: behold, he shall come, saith the LORD of hosts.

2 But who may abide the day of his coming? and who shall stand when he appeareth? for he is like a refiner's fire, and like fullers' soap:

3 And he shall sit as a refiner and purifier of silver: and he shall purify the sons of Levi, and purge them as gold and silver, that they may offer unto the LORD an offering in righteousness.

4 Then shall the offering of Judah and Jerusalem be pleasant unto the LORD, as in the days of old, and as in former years.

5 And I will come near to you to judgment; and I will be a swift witness against the sorcerers, and against the adulterers, and against false swearers, and against those that oppress the hireling in his wages, the widow, and the fatherless, and that turn aside the stranger from his right, and fear not me, saith the LORD of hosts.

6 For I am the LORD, I change not; therefore ye sons of Jacob are not consumed.

7 Even from the days of your fathers ye are gone away from mine ordinances, and have not kept them. Return unto me, and I will return unto you, saith the LORD of hosts. But ye said, Wherein shall we return?

8 Will a man rob God? Yet ye have robbed me. But ye say, Wherein have we robbed thee? In tithes and offerings.

9 Ye are cursed with a curse: for ye have robbed me, even this whole nation.

10 Bring ye all the tithes into the storehouse, that there may be meat in mine house, and prove me now herewith, saith the LORD of hosts, if I will not open you the windows of heaven, and pour you out a blessing, that there shall not be room enough to receive it.

LESSON 14 • AUGUST 31, 2025

BIBLICAL DEFINITIONS

A. **Purge** (Malachi 3:3) *zakak* (Heb.)—Purify, distill, strain, refine.

B. **Ordinance** (v. 7) *khok* (Heb.)—Civil enactment prescribed by God, a prescribed limit.

LIFE NEED FOR TODAY'S LESSON

AIM: Students will know that fairness and philanthropy are most apparent during times of great tragedy and loss.

INTRODUCTION
The Prophets Speak

Malachi was written during the post-exilic period. This was the time after the Jews returned from exile in Babylonia to rebuild their nation and the temple of God. Malachi was a contemporary of Zechariah and Haggai. All three prophets were concerned with the people's neglect and complacency concerning the worship of God and the people's repetition of the sins and injustice that caused them to be scattered in the first place. Malachi spoke out against a corrupt priesthood. He also indicted the people of Judah for their lack of faith, which was shown in the neglect of worship particularly in withholding tithes and sacrificial offerings. This meant that the priests who officiated worship were not adequately provided for. It also meant that worship was not continuous and therefore not a priority among the majority of the people. Malachi condemns this attitude and announces that God's messenger will come to refine His people so that they worship Him in righteousness.

BIBLE LEARNING

AIM: Students will know that God expects His people to be just, faithful, and show mercy.

I. The Messenger of God (Malachi 3:1–4)

Malachi begins this oracle with an announcement concerning God's messenger, who will prepare the way before Him. It is a prophecy concerning the time of the Messiah. The people needed to change their ways in order to receive the Messiah, so a messenger would be sent to prepare them for His coming. Although they longed for a Messiah who would bring justice, they were not in a moral state to be ready for Him. Malachi's announcement lets them know that a Messiah is coming, and they need to be ready for Him when He comes.

The Sovereign Ruler Returns (verses 1–4)

1 Behold, I will send my messenger, and he shall prepare the way before me: and the LORD, whom ye seek, shall suddenly come to his temple, even the messenger of the covenant, whom ye delight in: behold, he shall come, saith the LORD of hosts.

The name "Malachi" (Heb. *mal'aki*, **mal-ahKEE**) means "my messenger." However, scholars generally agree that the prophet who goes by that name is not being referred to here. The message that Malachi the prophet was to deliver to the people seems to be in response to their question in **Malachi 2:17** when they inquire, "Where is the God of Judgment?" Malachi responds that the Lord they were "seeking" (Heb. *baqash*, **bah-KASH**, to seek, demand, or find) and in whom they found "delight" (Heb. *chapets*, **khah-FAHTS**, having pleasure in) would come "suddenly" (Heb. *pitom*, **pith-OME**, any moment now or unexpectedly) to His temple. The question of those who were seeking to live and do right is rhetorical. The priests of the temple were corrupt and many of the people had stopped taking issues of right or wrong seriously. Malachi was warning that the Sovereign Ruler would come unannounced and would bring judgment with Him.

2 But who may abide the day of his coming? and who shall stand when he appeareth? for he is like a refiner's fire, and like fullers' soap:

Because the Lord would bring judgment with Him, Malachi asks the people, who will be able to "abide" (Heb. *kul*, **KOOL**, to survive or endure) the day "of his coming" (Heb. *bow'*, **BO**, to fall or light upon)? Further, he inquires who will be able to "stand" (Heb. *'amad*, **ahMAHD**, to stand up) when he "appeareth" (Heb. *ra'ah*, **rah-AH**, to present oneself or to be visible). The suggestion is that no one will be able to continue as before, because the Lord will come like a "refiner's" (Heb. *tsarap*, **tsahRAF**, to purge away or to smelt) fire or even like the "fuller's" (Heb. *kabas*, **kah-VAHS**, to launder or wash by treading) "soap" (Heb. *borit*, **bo-REETH**, lye or potash).

3 And he shall sit as a refiner and purifier of silver: and he shall purify the sons of Levi, and purge them as gold and silver, that they may offer unto the LORD an offering in righteousness. 4 Then shall the offering of Judah and Jerusalem be pleasant unto the LORD, as in the days of old, and as in former years.

Such a "purge" (Heb. *zaqaq*, **zah-KAHK**, to distill or strain) would be harsh on all who were found to be lacking moral or ethical standards. The Lord's purpose, once He appeared, would be to "purify" (Heb. *taher*, **tah-HAR**, to pronounce clean) His temple, and its leadership, the Levites. Malachi tells the people that the Lord would begin His work of purification with the priests. He would "sit" (Heb. *yashab*, **yah-SHAV**, to dwell or remain) as one who refines silver, because it is more difficult than refining gold. The refining of silver requires hotter fires and takes more time and patience. Once the temple and its leadership have been cleansed, the expectation is that the priests would once again return to the offering of sacrifices as spelled out in the laws of the Old Testament, and the people would follow their leadership. The end result of all of these actions would be a restoration of the relationship between God and His chosen people (see **Philippians 1:8–11**).

QUESTION 1
What is the purpose and role of the "messenger of the covenant" (**Malachi 3:2**)?.

II. THE MESSAGE OF GOD (vv. 5–7)
Malachi then takes the people into the heavenly law courts. The Lord is the chief witness testifying against them. He will not be hesitant but swift in His judgment of their unrighteousness. He has seen their adultery, oppression, sorcery, lying, and idolatry. They have no excuse for their behavior, and the Lord will see to it that they are judged accordingly. He then states, "I am the LORD, I change not." He is not a wishy-washy God. His character is steadfast and faithful, therefore they "are not consumed."

Judgment, Repentance, and Mercy (verses 5–7)

5 And I will come near to you to judgment; and I will be a swift witness against the sorcerers, and against the adulterers, and against false swearers, and against those that oppress the hireling in his wages, the widow, and the fatherless, and that turn aside the stranger from his right, and fear not me, saith the LORD of hosts. 6 For I am the LORD, I change not; therefore ye sons of Jacob are not consumed.

Malachi continues to respond to the people's question (**2:17**). He informs them that God will appear, and in addition to being a refining fire on some, will be the God of "judgment" (Heb. *mishpat*, **mish-PAHT**, justice, legal decision before a judge) they asked for. The continual presence of so many within the community of returned exiles practicing acts condemned by the Law served as an indication that they did not fear God and His punishment would be their reward. When God does appear to judge, there will be no need for others to be witnesses against the wrongdoers; God has declared that He Himself will be the witness. However, because God is unchanging and always remains true to His word, His people will not be "consumed" (Heb. *kalah*, **kah-LAH**, to come to an end) even in their faithlessness and rebellion.

7 Even from the days of your fathers ye are gone away from mine ordinances, and have not kept them. Return unto me, and I will return unto you, saith the LORD of hosts. But ye said, Wherein shall we return?

The rebellion in the Jewish nation had been going on for a very long time. Like their "fathers" (Heb. *'ab*, **AHV**, the head or founder of a household, group, family or clan) before them, the people had turned away from the ordinances of God and embraced the evil ways of men (see **Matthew 15:3**), which resulted in the ruin of the nation. Malachi, speaking for God, implores them to return to the "ordinances" (Heb. *choq*, **KHOKE**, rules or commands) of the Law so that the Lord of hosts would reward them by returning to them. The people have shown themselves deserving of God's wrath, and as the righteous judge, He had every right to consume them, but God demonstrates His patience and graciousness to His chosen people by speaking gently to them and offering for them to return. The people only needed to repent. This was the message of John the Baptist too (see **Matthew 3:2 and 4:17**). However, rather than repentance, the Lord's plea is met with continued denial and rebellion. The self-righteous Pharisees did not feel the need for repentance because they believed that they had kept the whole Law and were blameless before God. In asking "wherein they needed to return" (Heb. *shub*, **SHOOV**, to turn back) to God, they were justifying themselves and their behavior in their own eyes.

III. THE MAINTENANCE OF GOD'S HOUSE (vv. 8–10)

Malachi points out that they are the ones in the wrong. He pronounces them as cursed by the Lord. Although they demanded justice, they have robbed God by not giving the tithes of their crops and herds and by not giving the proper worship sacrifices or offerings (**Malachi 1:6–14**). They were giving blind, diseased, and sometimes even stolen animals to the temple. This was shameful and disrespectful in God's eyes. They also had not given the tithe, which was designed to support the priests and others who had no land rights (**Deuteronomy 14:28–29; 26:12**).

A Lack of Gratitude (verses 8–10)

8 Will a man rob God? Yet ye have robbed me. But ye say, Wherein have we robbed thee? In tithes and offerings. 9 Ye are cursed with a curse: for ye have robbed me, even this whole nation.

Through the prophet, God answers their inquiry. The people had become guilty of "robbing" (Heb. *qaba'*, **kah-VAH**, to defraud) God because they had stopped bringing their tithes and offerings for sacrifice to the temple. The nation was to take care of the needs of the priests and the Levites; however, by not giving their tithes and not offering sacrifices, or by doing either grudgingly, they were guilty of robbing God. The people's lack of giving with a cheerful spirit was viewed by God as a lack of gratitude for

LESSON 14 • AUGUST 31, 2025

how He favored them or lack of acknowledgement of Him as Lord. The "curse" (Heb. *'arar*, **ah-RAR**, to condemn or call judgment down on) God inflicted on them was the withholding of rain so their crops would not grow (see **3:11**).

10 Bring ye all the tithes into the storehouse, that there may be meat in mine house, and prove me now herewith, saith the LORD of hosts, if I will not open you the windows of heaven, and pour you out a blessing, that there shall not be room enough to receive it.

Finally, God challenges the people to put Him to the test. They are to once again bring their tithes to the "storehouse" (Heb. *'otsar*, **oh-TSAR**, treasure-house or armory), a repository which was attached to the temple and over which the priest exercised control, and "prove" (Heb. *bachan*, **bah-KHAN**, to examine or try) if God would in fact open the windows of heaven so that an overabundance of "blessing" (Heb. *berakah*, **beh-rah-KAH**, gift, prosperity) might flow down. Malachi suggests that the people who did bring tithes to the storehouse were guilty of withholding a portion of those tithes, thereby robbing God further. He implores the populace to bring all their tithes so that they might receive God's favor.

QUESTION 2
How could the people properly return to the Lord (v. 8–10)?

BIBLE APPLICATION
AIM: Students will give as a grateful expression of their commitment to God's grace and justice.

Many people today cry out hypocritically for justice. The same people who demand justice are quick to dish out injustice. We fight with others and look down on those who are disadvantaged. We cheat and steal from others in order to claw our way to success. Then we complain to God when someone cheats and steals from us. We are quick to point the finger and pray to God to make things right. We only pray when we need something and neglect God in our everyday life. The lesson for us today is that making things right has to start with us. We cannot think that God will take care of our house when we do not take care of His house.

STUDENTS' RESPONSES
AIM: Students will know believers confess their lack of forgiveness and seek human and divine forgiveness.

Oftentimes we want God to be there for us in our time of need, yet we don't ask how we can serve Him. This week in your prayer times, instead of asking the Lord for things that benefit you, ask Him how you can serve Him and be a blessing to those around you. If you are not being faithful in your financial giving to your local church, make a commitment to give. If you have been faithful, consider what charities or non-profits could be blessed by your financial giving. Ask your pastor or church leader whether there is a missionary you can help support through your financial contribution.

PRAYER
Lord, forgive us for not giving You the best that we have in our tithes, offerings, and our compassion for one another. Bless us to have the mind, heart, and spirit that is aligned with You commandments. In Jesus' name we pray. Amen.

Digging Deeper
Reflections on Tithes

There were various kinds of tithes and offerings required by the Mosaic law. The offerings were the first fruits of the harvest – at least one-sixtieth of the corn, wine, and oil (Deuteronomy 18:4).

There were at least four tithes:

1. A tenth of what remained after the first fruits were given to the priests went to support the Levites, who held no tribal territory.

    Every tithe of the land, whether of the seed of the land or of the fruits of the trees, is the Lord's; it is holy to the Lord (Leviticus 27:30).

2. The Levites, in turn, had to pay a tenth of their income to the priests.

    The Lord spoke to Moses, saying, "Moreover, you shall speak and say to the Levites, 'When you take from the people of Israel the tithe that I have given you from them for your inheritance, then you shall present a contribution from it to the Lord, a tithe of the tithe. And your contribution shall be counted to you as though it were the grain of the threshing floor and as the fullness of the winepress. So you shall also present a contribution to the Lord from all your tithes, which you receive from the people of Israel. And from it you shall give the Lord's contribution to Aaron the priest'" (Numbers 18:26-28).

3. A tithe was taken for the needs of the Levites who worked in connection with the tabernacle.

    You shall eat them [i.e., the tithe of your grain or of your wine or of your oil, or the firstborn of your herd or of your flock, or any of your vow offerings that you vow, or your freewill offerings of the contributions that you present (v. 17)] before the Lord your God in the place that the Lord your God will choose, you and your son and your daughter, your male servant and your female servant, and the Levite who is within your towns (Deuteronomy 12:18a).

4. Every third year, a special tithe is taken for the poor.

    At the end of every three years, you shall bring out all the tithe of your produce in the same year and lay it up within your towns. And the Levite, because he has no portion or inheritance with you, and the sojourner, that fatherless, and the widow, who are within your towns, shall come and eat and be filled that the Lord your God may bless you in all the work of your hands that you do (Deuteronomy 14:28-29)

Overall, we see that in Israel, tithing was a form of taxation to raise funds to support the religious establishment and finance social services.

HOW TO SAY IT

Sorcerer.	**SOR**-seh-rer.
Ordinance.	**OR**-di-nens.

LESSON 14 • AUGUST 31, 2025

DAILY HOME BIBLE READINGS

MONDAY
Teach Me Your Paths, O Lord
(Psalm 25)

TUESDAY
How Shall We Treat Others?
(Matthew 7:7–14)

WEDNESDAY
How Have We Spoken Against You?
(Malachi 3:11–18)

THURSDAY
How Shall We Be Judged?
(Joel 3:9–16)

FRIDAY
How Shall We Repent?
(Jeremiah 6:26–30)

SATURDAY
The Contrite and Humble in Spirit
(Isaiah 57:10–21)

SUNDAY
The Change Agent
(Malachi 3:1–10)

PREPARE FOR NEXT SUNDAY
Read **Acts 4:23–31** and study "Praying for One Another."

Sources:
Burton, James. *Coffman Commentaries on the Old Testament and New Testament*. Abilene, TX: Abilene Christian University Press, n.d.
Dunn, James D. G. and John W. Rogerson. *Commentary on the Bible*. Grand Rapids, MI: Wm. B. Eerdmans Publishing House, 2003.
Howley, G.C.D., F.F. Bruce, and H.L. Ellison. *The New Layman's Bible Commentary*. Grand Rapids, MI: Zondervan, 1979.

COMMENTS / NOTES:

The Symbol of the Church Of God In Christ

The Symbol of the Church Of God In Christ is an outgrowth of the Presiding Bishop's Coat of Arms, which has become quite familiar to the Church. The design of the Official Seal of the Church was created in 1973 and adopted in the General Assembly in 1981 (July Session).

The obvious GARNERED WHEAT in the center of the seal represents all of the people of the Church Of God In Christ, Inc. The ROPE of wheat that holds the shaft together represents the Founding Father of the Church, Bishop Charles Harrison Mason, who, at the call of the Lord, banded us together as a Brotherhood of Churches in the First Pentecostal General Assembly of the Church, in 1907.

The date in the seal has a two-fold purpose: first, to tell us that Bishop Mason received the baptism of the Holy Ghost in March 1907 and, second, to tell us that it was because of this outpouring that Bishop Mason was compelled to call us together in February of 1907 to organize the Church Of God In Christ.

The RAIN in the background represents the Latter Rain, or the End-time Revivals, which brought about the emergence of our Church along with other Pentecostal Holiness Bodies in the same era. The rain also serves as a challenge to the Church to keep Christ in the center of our worship and service, so that He may continue to use the Church Of God In Christ as one of the vehicles of Pentecostal Revival before the return of the Lord.

This information was reprinted from the book *So You Want to KNOW YOUR CHURCH* by Alferd Z. Hall, Jr.

COGIC AFFIRMATION OF FAITH

We believe the Bible to be the inspired and only infallible written Word of God.

We believe that there is One God, eternally existent in three Persons: God the Father, God the Son, and God the Holy Spirit.

We believe in the Blessed Hope, which is the rapture of the Church of God, which is in Christ at His return.

We believe that the only means of being cleansed from sin is through repentance and faith in the precious Blood of Jesus Christ.

We believe that regeneration by the Holy Ghost is absolutely essential for personal salvation.

We believe that the redemptive work of Christ on the Cross provides healing for the human body in answer to believing in prayer.

We believe that the baptism in the Holy Ghost, according to Acts 2:4, is given to believers who ask for it.

We believe in the sanctifying power of the Holy Spirit, by whose indwelling the Christian is enabled to live a Holy and separated life in this present world. Amen.

The Doctrines of the Church Of God In Christ

THE BIBLE

We believe that the Bible is the Word of God and contains one harmonious and sufficiently complete system of doctrine. We believe in the full inspiration of the Word of God. We hold the Word of God to be the only authority in all matters and assert that no doctrine can be true or essential if it does not find a place in this Word.

THE FATHER

We believe in God, the Father Almighty, the Author and Creator of all things. The Old Testament reveals God in diverse manners, by manifesting His nature, character, and dominions. The Gospels in the New Testament give us knowledge of God the "Father" or "My Father," showing the relationship of God to Jesus as Father, or representing Him as the Father in the Godhead, and Jesus himself that Son (St. John 15:8, 14:20). Jesus also gives God the distinction of "Fatherhood" to all believers when He explains God in the light of "Your Father in Heaven" (St. Matthew 6:8).

THE SON

We believe that Jesus Christ is the Son of God, the second person in the Godhead of the Trinity or Triune Godhead. We believe that Jesus was and is eternal in His person and nature as the Son of God who was with God in the beginning of creation (St. John 1:1). We believe that Jesus Christ was born of a virgin called Mary according to the Scripture (St. Matthew 1:18), thus giving rise to our fundamental belief in the Virgin

Birth and to all of the miraculous events surrounding the phenomenon (St. Matthew 1:18–25). We believe that Jesus Christ became the "suffering servant" to man; this suffering servant came seeking to redeem man from sin and to reconcile him to God, his Father (Romans 5:10). We believe that Jesus Christ is standing now as mediator between God and man (I Timothy 2:5).

THE HOLY GHOST

We believe the Holy Ghost or Holy Spirit is the third person of the Trinity; proceeds from the Father and the Son; is of the same substance, equal to power and glory; and is together with the Father and the Son, to be believed in, obeyed, and worshiped. The Holy Ghost is a gift bestowed upon the believer for the purpose of equipping and empowering the believer, making him or her a more effective witness for service in the world. He teaches and guides one into all truth (John 16:13; Acts 1:8, 8:39).

THE BAPTISM OF THE HOLY GHOST

We believe that the Baptism of the Holy Ghost is an experience subsequent to conversion and sanctification and that tongue-speaking is the consequence of the baptism in the Holy Ghost with the manifestations of the fruit of the spirit (Galatians 5:22–23; Acts 10:46, 19:1–6). We believe that we are not baptized with the Holy Ghost in order to be saved (Acts 19:1–6; John 3:5). When one receives a baptismal Holy Ghost experience, we believe one will speak with a tongue unknown to oneself according to the sovereign will of Christ. To be filled with the Spirit means to be Spirit controlled as expressed by Paul in Ephesians 5:18,19. Since the charismatic demonstrations were necessary to help the early church to be successful in implementing the command of Christ, we, therefore, believe that a Holy Ghost experience is mandatory for all believers today.

MAN

We believe that humankind was created holy by God, composed of body, soul, and spirit. We believe that humankind, by nature, is sinful and unholy. Being born in sin, a person needs to be born again, sanctified and cleansed from all sins by the blood of Jesus. We believe that one is saved by confessing and forsaking one's sins, and believing on the Lord Jesus Christ, and that having become a child of God, by being born again and adopted into the family of God, one may, and should, claim the inheritance of the sons of God, namely the baptism of the Holy Ghost.

SIN

Sin, the Bible teaches, began in the angelic world (Ezekiel 28:11–19; Isaiah 14:12–20) and is transmitted into the blood of the human race through disobedience and deception motivated by unbelief (I Timothy 2:14). Adam's sin, committed by eating of the forbidden fruit from the tree of knowledge of good and evil, carried with it permanent pollution or depraved human nature to all his descendants. This is called "original sin." Sin can now be defined as a volitional transgression against God and a lack of conformity to the will of God. We, therefore, conclude that humankind by nature is sinful and has fallen from a glorious and righteous state from which we were created, and has become unrighteous and unholy. We therefore, must be restored to the state of holiness from which we have fallen by being born again (St. John 3:7).

SALVATION

Salvation deals with the application of the work of redemption to the sinner with restoration to divine favor and communion with God. This redemptive operation of the Holy Ghost upon sinners is brought about by repentance toward God and faith toward our Lord Jesus Christ which brings conversion, faith, justification, regeneration, sanctification, and the baptism of the Holy Ghost. Repentance is the work of God, which results in a change of mind in respect to a person's relationship to God (St. Matthew 3:1–2, 4:17; Acts 20:21). Faith is a certain conviction wrought in the heart by the Holy Spirit, as to the truth of the Gospel and a heart trust in the promises of God in Christ (Romans 1:17, 3:28; St. Matthew 9:22; Acts 26:18). Conversion is that act of God whereby He causes the regenerated sinner, in one's conscious life, to turn to Him in repentance and faith (II Kings 5:15; II Chronicles 33:12,13; St. Luke 19:8,9; Acts 8:30). Regeneration is the act of God by which the principle of the new life is implanted in humankind, the governing disposition of soul is made holy, and the first holy exercise of this new disposition is secured. Sanctification is that gracious and continuous operation of the Holy Ghost, by which He delivers the justified sinner from the pollution of sin, renews a person's whole nature in the image of God, and enables one to perform good works (Romans 6:4, 5:6; Colossians 2:12, 3:1).

ANGELS

The Bible uses the term "angel" (a heavenly body) clearly and primarily to denote messengers or ambassadors of God with such Scripture references as Revelations 4:5, which indicates their duty in heaven to praise God (Psalm 103:20), to do God's will (St. Matthew 18:10), and to behold His face. But since heaven must come down to earth, they also have a mission to earth. The Bible indicates that they accompanied God in the Creation, and also that they will accompany Christ in His return in Glory.

DEMONS

Demons denote unclean or evil spirits; they are sometimes called devils or demonic beings. They are evil spirits, belonging to the unseen or spiritual realm, embodied in human beings. The Old Testament refers to the prince of demons, sometimes called Satan (adversary) or Devil, as having power and wisdom, taking the habitation of other forms such as the serpent (Genesis 3:1). The New Testament speaks of the Devil as Tempter (St. Matthew 4:3), and it goes on to tell the works of

Satan, the Devil, and demons as combating righteousness and good in any form, proving to be an adversary to the saints. Their chief power is exercised to destroy the mission of Jesus Christ. It can well be said that the Christian Church believes in demons, Satan, and devils. We believe in their power and purpose. We believe they can be subdued and conquered as in the commandment to the believer by Jesus. "In my name they shall cast out Satan and the work of the Devil and to resist him and then he will flee (WITHDRAW) from you" (St. Mark 16:17).

THE CHURCH

The Church forms a spiritual unity of which Christ is the divine head. It is animated by one Spirit, the Spirit of Christ. It professes one faith, shares one hope, and serves one King. It is the citadel of the truth and God's agency for communicating to believers all spiritual blessings. The Church then is the object of our faith rather than of knowledge. The name of our Church, "CHURCH OF GOD IN CHRIST," is supported by I Thessalonians 2:14 and other passages in the Pauline Epistles. The word "CHURCH" or "EKKLESIA" was first applied to the Christian society by Jesus Christ in St. Matthew 16:18, the occasion being that of His benediction of Peter at Caesarea Philippi.

THE SECOND COMING OF CHRIST

We believe in the second coming of Christ; that He shall come from heaven to earth, personally, bodily, visibly (Acts 1:11; Titus 2:11–13; St. Matthew 16:27, 24:30, 25:30; Luke 21:27; John 1:14, 17; Titus 2:11); and that the Church, the bride, will be caught up to meet Him in the air (I Thessalonians 4:16–17). We admonish all who have this hope to purify themselves as He is pure.

DIVINE HEALING

The Church Of God In Christ believes in and practices Divine Healing. It is a commandment of Jesus to the Apostles (St. Mark 16:18). Jesus affirms His teachings on healing by explaining to His disciples, who were to be Apostles, that healing the afflicted is by faith (St. Luke 9:40–41). Therefore, we believe that healing by faith in God has scriptural support and ordained authority. St. James's writings in his epistle encourage Elders to pray for the sick, lay hands upon them and to anoint them with oil, and state that prayers with faith shall heal the sick and the Lord shall raise them up. Healing is still practiced widely and frequently in the Church Of God In Christ, and testimonies of healing in our Church testify to this fact.

MIRACLES

The Church Of God In Christ believes that miracles occur to convince people that the Bible is God's Word. A miracle can be defined as an extraordinary visible act of divine power, wrought by the efficient agency of the will of God, which has as its final cause the vindication of the righteousness of God's Word. We believe that the works of God, which were performed during the beginnings of Christianity, do and will occur even today where God is preached, faith in Christ is exercised, the Holy Ghost is active, and the Gospel is promulgated in the truth (Acts 5:15, 6:8, 9:40; Luke 4:36, 7:14, 15, 5:5, 6; St. Mark 14:15).

THE ORDINANCES OF THE CHURCH

It is generally admitted that for an ordinance to be valid, it must have been instituted by Christ. When we speak of ordinances of the church, we are speaking of those instituted by Christ, in which by sensible signs the grace of God in Christ and the benefits of the covenant of grace are represented, sealed, and applied to believers, and these in turn give expression to their faith and allegiance to God. The Church Of God In Christ recognizes three ordinances as having been instituted by Christ himself and, therefore, are binding upon the church practice.

THE LORD'S SUPPER (HOLY COMMUNION)

The Lord's Supper symbolizes the Lord's death and suffering for the benefit and in the place of His people. It also symbolizes the believer's participation in the crucified Christ. It represents not only the death of Christ as the object of faith, which unites the believers to Christ, but also the effect of this act as the giving of life, strength, and joy to the soul. The communicant by faith enters into a special spiritual union of one's soul with the glorified Christ.

FOOT WASHING

Foot washing is practiced and recognized as an ordinance in our Church because Christ, by His example, showed that humility characterized greatness in the kingdom of God, and that service rendered to others gave evidence that humility, motivated by love, exists. These services are held subsequent to the Lord's Supper; however, its regularity is left to the discretion of the pastor in charge.

WATER BAPTISM

We believe that Water Baptism is necessary as instructed by Christ in St. John 3:5, "UNLESS MAN BE BORN AGAIN OF WATER AND OF THE SPIRIT..."

However, we do not believe that water baptism alone is a means of salvation, but is an outward demonstration that one has already had a conversion experience and has accepted Christ as his personal Savior. As Pentecostals, we practice immersion in preference to sprinkling because immersion corresponds more closely to the death, burial, and resurrection of our Lord (Colossians 2:12). It also symbolizes regeneration and purification more than any other mode. Therefore, we practice immersion as our mode of baptism. We believe that we should use the Baptismal Formula given to us by Christ for all "...IN THE NAME OF THE FATHER, AND OF THE SON, AND OF THE HOLY GHOST..." (Matthew 28:19).

Suggested Order of Service

Call to order.

Singing.

Prayer.

New Responsive Reading & Core Values

ISSD: Responsive Reading

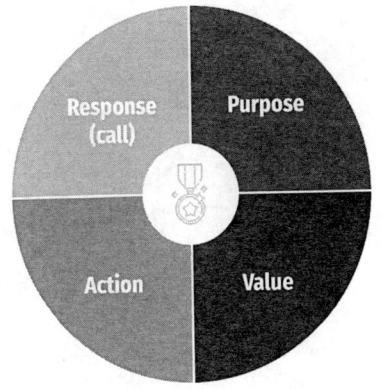

Calls for the response of worship of God
Calls for response to God (in unity)
Calls for response to God's truth

Builds identity around our core values
Builds student belief in themselves and in the mission of The Church

- To support students in achieving the curricular outcomes
- To inspire students to become engaged in comprehension and practice of scriptural commands

- For the life of The Church, it is:
  -biblical
  -historic
  -participatory
  -instructional

Suggested Order of Service

Responsive reading continued:

Sunday School's Core Values

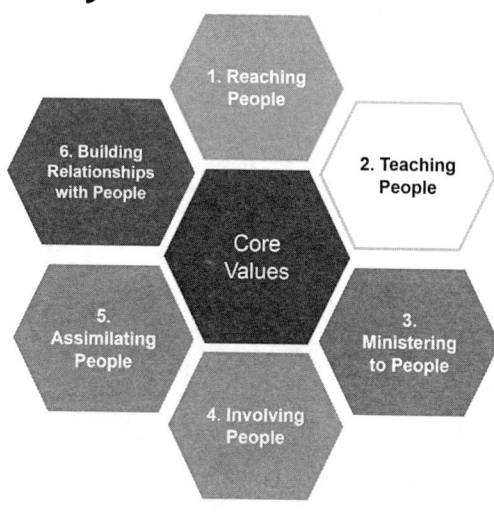

Core Values in Detail

01	02	03	04	05	06
Reaching People	**Teaching People**	**Ministering to People**	**Involving People**	**Assimilating People**	**Building Relationships**
We believe that Sunday School should have a two-fold focus: sharing the gospel and teaching biblical principles for life application.	We believe that recruiting and developing leaders is top priority.	We believe that this can be accomplished by creating care groups within the Sunday School.	We believe that Sunday School should equip and give every member an opportunity to serve Christ.	We teach that getting visitors and new members involved in Sunday School is the best way to keep them in the Church.	We believe that relationships are one of the main reasons why people attend Sunday School.

new RESPONSIVE READING

SUPERINTENDENT/TEACHER: Behold how good and how pleasant it is for brethren to dwell together in unity! *Psalm 133:1*

SCHOOL/CLASS: But to do good and to communicate forget not: for with such sacrifices God is well pleased. *Hebrews 13:16*

SUPERINTENDENT/TEACHER: All scripture is given by inspiration of God, and is profitable for doctrine, for reproof, for correction, for instruction in righteousness. *2 Timothy 3:16*

SCHOOL/CLASS: Thy word is a lamp unto my feet, and a light unto my path. *Psalm 119:105*

SUPERINTENDENT/TEACHER: Look not every man on his own things, but every man also on the things of others. *Philippians 2:4*

SCHOOL/CLASS: He that hath a bountiful eye shall be blessed; for he giveth of his bread to the poor. *Proverbs 22:9*

SUPERINTENDENT/TEACHER: Wherefore he saith, When he ascended up on high, he led captivity captive, and gave gifts unto men. *Ephesians 4:8*

SCHOOL/CLASS: As every man hath received the gift, even so minister the same one to another, as good stewards of the manifold grace of God. *1 Peter 4:10*

SUPERINTENDENT/TEACHER: For as the body is one, and hath many members, and all the members of that one body, being many, are one body: so also is Christ. *1 Corinthians 12:12*

SCHOOL/CLASS: For as we have many members in one body, and all members have not the same office. *Romans 12:4*

SUPERINTENDENT/TEACHER: By this shall all men know that ye are my disciples, if ye have love one to another. *John 13:35*

SCHOOL/CLASS: For, brethren, ye have been called unto liberty; only use not liberty for an occasion to the flesh, but by love serve one another. *Galatians 5:13*

SUPERINTENDENT/ALL: But grow in grace, and in the knowledge of our Lord and Saviour Jesus Christ. To him be glory both now and for ever. Amen. *2 Peter 3:18*

Notes